THE FACTS

THE
NAPOLEONIC
WARS
IN 100
FACTS

JEM DUDUCU

Dedicated to Inji, Kathy, Alex and Delphi: this book so isn't you, but you get the dedication because you are all so important to me.

First published 2015

Amberley Publishing
The Hill, Stroud
Gloucestershire, GL5 4EP

www.amberley-books.com

British Library Cataloguing in Publication Data.
A catalogue record for this book is available from the British Library.

ISBN 978 1 4456 4663 3 (paperback)
ISBN 978 1 4456 4664 0 (ebook)

Typeset in 11pt on 13.5pt Sabon.
Typesetting and Origination by Amberley Publishing.
Printed in the UK.

Introduction

The war from 1914 to 1918 is sometimes called the Great War but is far more often known as the First World War. This is odd because the whole world wasn't involved, and neither was the whole world fighting in the Second World War. What these two conflicts have in common were battles that occurred in far-flung places and mass destruction in Europe. So if those factors define 'world war', there have been many more than just two.

The wars that France fought after the French Revolution, which continued for about a quarter of a century and ended at Waterloo, are among the earliest 'world wars'. Napoleon himself would fight on three continents, and Wellington fought on two. As you will see, there was fighting in both North and South America, on the tempestuous Atlantic, in the shadow of the pyramids and on the freezing steppes of Russia. This was an era when national borders were altered and political landscapes changed forever.

Much like the more famous later world wars, the Napoleonic Wars also marked an end to many of the 'old ways'. While the fighting was truly epic, so were the social changes in Britain and throughout Europe. Some of the institutions created in the Middle Ages had lasted into the Age of Enlightenment but were finally moved into the pages of history with the close of this period. The eventual hard-won victory over Napoleon gave the British Empire further impetus to expand manufacturing, create new technologies and become the first industrialised nation in the world.

The topic then is broad, spanning decades and continents. You can find hundreds of books on these wars; some manage to spin out just one battle into 400 pages, so a newcomer can feel a little daunted. This book is the antidote to that problem; in just 100 facts you will get an overview of the most important people, battles and events of this turbulent era.

Because of the time span, titles often changed; therefore, terms such as 'general' are used for expediency. The person in question at any particular battle or event may have been, specifically, a marshal or lieutenant colonel, but the broader point is that he was there in his capacity as a leader. It's also worth mentioning that exact numbers of troops or casualties are always up for debate. I tend to go for a reasonable average. In short, please remember that this book is a convenient summary of complex politics and countless battles.

This period was partially covered in *The British Empire in 100 Facts*; however, this book provides considerably more information about these twenty-five key years in European history. If a topic was raised in the previous book, it will be looked at from a new angle in this one.

If you are a history boffin who knows your Aboukir from your Austerlitz, then you are unlikely to find anything new here. This is a light, fast-paced introduction to the topic. You can read a few facts at a time or gorge on the whole lot in one go; it's up to you. But I hope you have as much pleasure reading this as I had writing it.

1. THE TRIGGER FOR WAR WAS THE FRENCH REVOLUTION

Revolting against an autocratic regime was nothing new in the eighteenth century, nor was the idea of overthrowing a monarchy. Athens had been a democracy, Rome had been a republic and the English Civil War had seen Parliament kill a king.

However, since the Age of Enlightenment – an era of philosophical and scientific blossoming centred in the mid-eighteenth century – the intelligentsia of most countries realised there might be better ways to run a country than gambling on the ruler's son being a competent replacement.

In France the initial stages of the revolution in 1789–90 saw these enlightenment ideals support a peasant uprising against crippling taxes and a feudal system that had changed little over the centuries. However, as William Pitt the Elder put it in 1770, 'Unlimited power is apt to corrupt the minds of those who possess it.' So as a new political system began to emerge, there was a scramble for power, and it was the radicals who won.

It was 1792–93 when things went horribly wrong for everyone. The radicals not only feared the other monarchies of Europe, they also wanted to export their revolutionary ideas. This led to a declaration of war against Austria, and Austria and Prussia went to war with France. The French leaders were big on ideas but small in their abilities to manage government. The early revolutionary armies of France were poorly equipped, so it was only thanks to some talented generals that they were able to get more out of their forces than was expected. France was saved from invasion, but that war would become known as the war that started what today we call the Napoleonic Wars – even though, in 1792, Napoleon was an insignificant junior officer.

It was in 1793 that a sense of existential threat manifested itself in the rest of Europe's royal houses. Aristocrats had already been beheaded by guillotine in front of cheering crowds, but in January of that year, Louis XVI was executed. Nothing like this had happened since the time of Charles I in England, about 150 years earlier. It sent shockwaves across the courts of Europe.

Then there was the 'Reign of Terror' under Robespierre. This was another violent conflict between revolutionary factions that led to what was estimated to be more than 40,000 executions. France was veering into bloody anarchy, and it was time the rest of Europe did everyone a favour by trying to sort it out.

It's that final point that's important. Many people regard the Second World War as a 'just war', one where the Allies had moral right on their side. The same can be said for this war. The powers of Europe did not want to conquer France, just stop the murderous rampages. As France felt justifiably threatened, it lashed out at all the nations it could and did so with amazing efficiency. This was the base cause of war for a quarter of a century.

2. The First Coalition Was Meant to Be the Only One

The French Revolutionary Wars and the Napoleonic Wars are split by most historians into different phases of warfare with different coalitions. At the time of the First Coalition, it was hoped that this would be the solution to France's revolutionary wars, but it was to be only the first of many such political alliances.

What this meant, in practical terms, was that while France regularly fought Austria, Prussia and Britain, other nations, such as Russia, would drift in and out of the story of this conflict or even, at times, change sides.

The War of the First Coalition lasted from the outbreak of hostilities in 1792 to 1797. France, at first, stood alone but over this period managed to gain allies with some Italian states (which had been conquered by the French), Northern Europe, Batavia and some areas of Poland. Spain is the most interesting country of this era because the monarchy had every reason to fight against France and did so up until 1796, but it was then persuaded to switch sides.

The First Coalition consisted of Austria, Britain, Prussia, the Netherlands, Naples and Sicily as well as some Italian states (not conquered by the French) and, as previously stated, Spain (at least for a while). Things get even murkier because Prussia was forced out of the war in 1795. The coalitions were therefore constantly mutating, although the differences between the First Coalition and later coalitions were fairly minimal. It was almost inevitably the German nations and Britain regularly clashing with France and Spain.

Communication was a major problem in an era when orders were sent by letter. Meetings would take weeks to arrange, and key decisions took days as the need for clarifications required messages to be exchanged with those in the home country, and final agreements needed the assent of far-off rulers, hundreds of miles away.

While alliances could agree certain principles and goals, regular strategic updates were impossible. If, for example, Austria was at risk of defeat, it would be too late for any of the other powers to change their plans and help an ally in need.

Military campaigns were confined to one season mainly because armies lived off the land, which meant foraging for food in winter would be difficult, and it was very hard to maintain a large force in such situations. The alliances of this era tended to come up with a broad strategy for the campaigning season, reconvene at the end of it to see how things had gone and then set the goals for the coming year.

With such a system in place, it is easy to see how the idea of war became an extension of politics, and how whole campaigns were based on little more than a 'gentleman's agreement'. And yet these decisions, made in drawing rooms far from the field of battle, were to affect hundreds of thousands of lives. It was never meant to be callous; it was just how things were done.

3. KING GEORGE III WASN'T AS MAD AS YOU MIGHT THINK

It was the English Civil War in the 1640s that tipped the balance of power away from the monarchy towards Parliament. 150 years later, the advantages of having a government with real power were to become abundantly clear.

The main issue with any monarchy is its unreliability; it's a gamble. Just because one ruler is competent does not guarantee the heirs will be too, and because they are divinely anointed when crowned, the only way to get rid of them is through bloody civil war. However, parliamentary democracy stopped all that, which was fortuitous because George III would have been a terrible ruler had he been an absolute monarch.

George III came to the throne in the middle of the Seven Years' War, which propelled Britain from its role as an imperial rival to France to the most powerful empire in the world. However, George was still king during the American Revolution, which saw Britain lose its colonies. Now Britain faced a revolutionary France in a war that would end up being fought for more than two decades. It is therefore fortunate that George, who was king for nearly sixty years, was little more than a figurehead because he had a habit of lapsing into melancholy and insane delusions.

George hadn't always been like this, and during the first few decades of his reign, he was energetic in his regal duties and a good public speaker. He was also the first of the Hanoverian dynasty to actually have been born in Britain, which bound him more closely to his subjects. As kings go, he was loved.

However, in 1788, he suffered from a bout of

porphyria, a rare mental illness that is thought to have been brought on from his exposure to arsenic (not by being intentionally poisoned but probably via the cosmetics and medicines of the day). This was twenty-eight years into his reign, and he did recover; however, episodes of mental illness after this were to become more and more frequent. While images of him usually show a slim man in a red tunic, wearing the customary white wig of the era, an engraving of him in 1811 shows a fat, sallow man with long hair and a beard, unrecognisable as the younger George.

George not only suffered from porphyria but cataracts too, and by 1811 he was virtually blind. It was at this stage that the Regency Act was passed, an Act that made his decadent and profligate embarrassment of a son (later, George IV) the Prince Regent. The king and his son were very different men, but even taking into account the king's health, the prince was hardly an improvement on his father. Had these two been responsible for British military planning in the later stages of this war, defeat would have been all but guaranteed. However, Parliament acted as a safety net, and far more capable men ran the country and steered the nation away from disaster.

4. THE YOUNG NAPOLEON SHOWED NO PROMISE

The Bonapartes (Buonapartes in Italian) had originated in Italy, but Napoleon was born into a branch of the family that moved to Corsica. His parents were both of minor Corsican nobility and had married young. The couple had had another son called Napoleon four years before the more famous one, but the earlier child died in infancy. Growing up in Corsica, Napoleon's first language was Italian; however, as his family was well off (by Corsican standards), he and his brother Joseph were shipped off to military academies in France.

Napoleon did not fit in particularly well. While he did learn French, he spoke it with an accent that betrayed his roots, and he was teased for sounding like a peasant. Also, the other boys came from well-connected and more affluent families. They were good at dancing; he was good at gardening. It was not a promising start for a boy who, at various times, dreamed of becoming an officer in the French navy or an artillery instructor in the Ottoman Empire. How different history would have been had he taken one of those (not unreasonable) routes.

Aged fifteen, Napoleon was admitted to the elite École Militaire in Paris. This was a huge honour, which turned into a disaster when his father died of stomach cancer while he was in his first year. The young cadet was now expected to be the family's chief income earner at the same time as he was attending one of the most expensive schools in France. The situation forced him to complete the two-year course in just one, and while he came only forty-second in a class of fifty-eight, graduation meant he could become a commissioned officer just after his sixteenth birthday. The year 1785 had no intake for the navy, so Napoleon joined an artillery unit (his mathematics was always good, so this was a natural fit) and became a second lieutenant in 1786.

In 1788, Napoleon took his eleven-year-old brother, Louis, into his care and, for the next few years, spent more time out of the army on leave than he spent on his military duties. Some of this time was devoted to schooling Louis, but Napoleon was also involved in the fight for Corsican independence and dedicated much of this period to campaigning for it. Certainly in his youth Napoleon did not consider himself to be French. As we will see, his loyalty to his family led to some spectacularly poor choices later in his career.

By 1791, as war was about to break out across Europe, Napoleon, still a second lieutenant stationed in a sleepy garrison town, went on leave to see his family in Corsica. This was about as unexceptional a start to a military career as can be imagined. No one could have predicted that, within ten years, he would be the most feared military commander in Europe – and, later, would become one of the greatest generals in history.

5. VALMY WAS THE FIRST OF MANY BATTLES

In the summer of 1792, enough was enough for Prussia and Austria. Both countries raised armies with the intention of stifling the revolutionary zealots of France and restoring order by placing the French king back on the throne. Initial skirmishes showed that while the revolutionaries had plenty of spirit, they were poorly equipped and had little training.

However, the revolutionaries still had a core of old troops and generals. In particular, Dumouriez and Kellermann were still around. Dumouriez (Fact 7) was an experienced war minister and had been manoeuvring to get himself into a position where he could lead an army, and Kellermann had seen active service in Poland. They were to become an effective team.

Meanwhile, the Austro-Prussian army had pushed through Verdun and on into the Forest of Argonne. It was heading straight for Paris with a sizeable force of 30,000–35,000. Dumouriez had been heading north towards the Netherlands but quickly turned his forces back, and he and Kellerman were able to get behind the invading force.

While in theory the army could have continued onwards to Paris, their lines of communication and supply were now cut, so the French had to be dealt with. The Austro-Prussian force turned away from Paris and met the French at Valmy. The terrain was hilly, with areas of thick forest, and both sides had roughly equal forces. It would be a strategic game of cat and mouse.

Dumouriez had manoeuvred the army to the planned area, while Kellermann got to the high ground with his artillery. Having positioned himself in a windmill, Kellerman was able to command withering fire on the Prussian troops, who advanced past the tree line of the forest. The Prussians replied by bringing up their cannon, but Kellermann's troops were largely French army regulars and knew what they were doing. The French won the artillery duel, and the Austro-Prussian infantry advance wavered.

It was at this point that Kellermann took his hat off and shouted, 'Vive la Nation!' This cry was taken up by the troops, and as the French poured down from the top of the slope, the invaders panicked, and the panic tuned into a rout. The Austro-Prussians turned tail and fled ... and then an unusually intense rain storm broke, lashing the miserable retreating troops and further crushing their morale.

While the French plan had been sound, the fighting had been expected to be harder. As it was, Valmy was a decisive victory for France and stopped the revolutionary government, still in its infancy, from being strangled in the cradle. The revolutionary propagandists called it a miracle, and it became a much-hyped engagement; but had the French been defeated, it could well have ended the French Revolution in a single battle. Total casualties were less than 500. The rest of the war would be far bloodier.

At Valmy today, there is a statue of Kellermann raising his hat and shouting his cry.

6. THERE WERE MANY TYPES OF CAVALRY

One of the difficulties in discussing the Napoleonic Wars is the number of military terms not in use today. Perhaps the area which best shows this is that relating to the different types of cavalry.

For example, there were the Cuirassiers: these were riders who wore an armoured breast plate (called a *cuirass* in French) and sometimes a steel helmet. They were the last remnants of the armoured knights of old, and while a well-aimed musket could puncture their armour, a glancing shot and pistol fire were largely ineffectual. They were a type of heavy cavalry.

Then there were the Carabiniers: these were horse-mounted riflemen armed with carbines. A carbine (jargon alert) was a shortened version of an infantry firearm and therefore thought to be less cumbersome for the men of the cavalry to use.

The Hussars may be a familiar term: these were a type of light cavalry. With no armour and no carbines, these cavalry men were all about manoeuvrability. Mounted on fast horses, they were often used for scouting and, in battle, would use curved sabres.

Finally, there were the Dragoons: originally mounted infantry (i.e. they would ride into battle, then dismount), by the nineteenth century they had become another form of light cavalry. They were slightly heavier than the Hussars because they often had larger horses and wore helmets. They were a particular favourite of Napoleon's, although, as will be seen later, Britain used them to good effect too.

7. Charles Dumouriez Had Many Ups and Downs

Charles Dumouriez has already been mentioned in Fact 5 about the Battle of Valmy, and in a way, he is a microcosm of the complexity of the era. While Napoleon would come to define these wars, in 1792 he wasn't even a minor player. Instead, the protection of the French Republic was the responsibility of generals like Dumouriez, who have been largely forgotten.

As a young officer, Dumouriez had fought in the Seven Years' War and spent the next few decades as a diplomat and as Secretary of State for War. This was all at Versailles, the court of the French kings, but he effortlessly changed sides and became a revolutionary commander (with the added benefit of keeping his head). Most revolutions keep some of the old guard; they are too useful and too experienced for them all to be imprisoned or executed.

On the one hand, Dumouriez was a revolutionary and was obsessed with spreading French revolutionary values to Belgium; on the other hand, he put up a spirited defence against the execution of Louis XVI. He was a great revolutionary hero after Valmy, and he received a rapturous welcome on his return to Paris.

It is interesting to note that his defence of the king was not what brought about his downfall. Instead, it was the far more practical matter of underachievement. His obsession with spreading revolution to Belgium led to an invasion in late 1792. Dumouriez won a battle and made rapid progress into the country. However, in March of 1793, he fought an Austrian and Dutch army at Neerwinden and suffered a major defeat.

In every sense of the word, that battle was a

disaster for Dumouriez. Not only did wave after wave of his men get slaughtered and pushed back in an unimaginative display of leadership (or lack of it), but the defeat led to a collapse of French power in Belgium. All he had gained was now lost. Dumouriez knew the sharks were circling, and he returned to Paris in an attempt to round up his critics and imprison them. His attempt at a coup completely failed, and he was forced to flee into the arms of his enemy.

In the space of one year, Dumouriez had gone from hero to pariah in France. He then spent more than a decade travelling from country to country, trying to avoid capture by Napoleon's far-reaching advances into neighbouring states and beyond.

In 1804, he decided to settle in England. The British government gave him a pension, and he became an advisor to the British war effort against Napoleon, proving himself to be of great value. When Louis XVIII was installed as the French king, Dumouriez tried to return to France as a marshal, but it came to nothing. He died in Henley in 1823.

When it comes to military leadership after the revolution, Dumouriez's career is a reminder that Napoleon arrived late to the game.

8. THE GRAND OLD DUKE OF YORK WAS NOT SO GRAND

The well-known song 'The Grand Old Duke of York, he had 10,000 men ...' has a long history, and the lyrics have been changed over time. The earliest version seems to have sprung up during the English Civil War era, but the more commonly sung lyrics about an ineffectual military commander with a lot of troops seem to be based on Prince Frederick, Duke of York and Albany.

Frederick was the second son of George III and was just about as useless as his older brother, the Prince Regent, later George IV, known for being a womaniser, a profligate spender and a compulsive gambler. He was also fat and lazy – not the most noble summary of a monarch.

As the heir presumptive, Frederick followed a traditional path of service in the military. While perhaps not as indolent or as decadent in his private life as his brother (the Prince Regent really did take these vices to a new low), he was in a position to cause far more harm, and his failings affected far more people: he was a poor leader put in charge of thousands of troops.

The best-known version of the song comes from his leadership of British forces in the War of the First Coalition against the French in the 1790s. His first mission in Flanders resulted in a failed siege and two minor defeats in battle, followed by withdrawal. Then in 1794, he returned to Flanders at the head of an army but not as overall leader.

This time he managed to capture a few Dutch ships and manoeuvre his forces in such a way that they were never attacked – nor did much attacking. This was one of the dullest campaigns in military history. Frederick then signed the Convention of Alkmaar, which led to an exchange of prisoners, and withdrew from Flanders – again.

Frederick's inaction and overcautious leadership were a reflection of the fact that Britain's standing army was tiny compared to the forces of states like Austria and France. Britannia may have ruled the waves, but on the land ... not so much. The Flanders campaign is a sobering reminder that the British army had a long way to go if it ever hoped to challenge French military superiority in Europe.

To Frederick's credit, he understood this and supported military reforms to improve not only the logistics of the army but also the quality of its officers. This plan manifested itself in 1801, when he backed the creation of Sandhurst (now Britain's leading military academy), which worked on merit rather than social position. Frederick was never to see a field of battle again (probably for the best) and died peacefully in bed in 1827.

Going back to the song, the lines about tedious marching around hills reflect the duke's dull manoeuvring in Flanders. That's perhaps a little unfair, but the song ensures that he is, at least, remembered.

9. War Had Many Colours

Two distinguishing features of warfare in this era are the bright uniforms and the rigid formations of the armies.

Today, camouflage and small unit tactics are vital, but modern armies have the advantages of air strikes, automatic weapons and rifles accurate for hundreds of meters. None of this was true in the eighteenth and nineteenth centuries. Muskets and cannon caused huge amounts of smoke to stream over battlefields, and the time needed for slow-loading firearms meant that lines of men firing in volleys were the only effective way to stop an enemy advance.

With this in mind, tight formations were vital. Lines were used when one group of infantry blasted away at other infantry. If attacked by cavalry, soldiers would form squares. Less overall firepower could be ranged, but the cavalry couldn't outflank this formation of soldiers, their bayonets bristling like a steel hedgehog.

In all the confusion of battle, troops needed to understand who was on which side. It was a matter of life and death to know if the battalion moving to your left flank were compatriots, allies or the enemy. So, rather helpfully, every country had its own colour scheme. The French wore dark blue jackets with white trousers; the British had their red coats (allegedly to disguise the extent of wounds); the Prussians wore black or Prussian Blue (the first mass-produced synthetic colour) and the Austrians were in white. Battles of the era were a maelstrom of colour.

10. A Private Became a Marshal of France

Jean-Baptiste Jourdan joined the French army as a private in 1778. He fought in the American War of Independence, served in the West Indies and was discharged after falling ill, probably with malaria. Following his short military career, he went home to Limoges, where he set up a haberdashery business and led a quiet life until the French Revolution.

When the new National Assembly asked for volunteers, Jourdan enlisted and was given a division – a huge leap forwards in terms of rank. But Jourdan rose to the challenge and, in 1792, won the Battle of Jemappes. He was also one of the commanding officers at the battle at Neerwinden, but as that was Dumouriez's debacle, Jourdan wasn't closely associated with the defeat. Yet again, we see a French general fighting multiple battles at a time when Napoleon was not yet part of the story.

In 1793, the French besieged Dunkirk. When the Anglo-Dutch army marched to relieve the beleaguered town, Jourdan met and defeated it at the Battle of Hondschoote (although he was wounded in the chest in one of the charges). It was a French victory, and Dunkirk fell to the French. However, Houchard, the other French general at the battle, failed to pursue the enemy; he was recalled, then tried and executed for cowardice. Again, although Jourdan's co-leader fell from grace, he himself had proved to be an excellent battlefield commander.

In 1794, his target was the city of Charleroi in Belgium. As he approached the city, he was forced to turn back by the Austrians. Immediately he manoeuvred his forces to come at the city from an unexpected direction – and took it quickly.

In 1795, after a long siege, he captured Luxembourg, and in 1796, he and other French forces were pushing beyond the Rhine. This advance was finally halted, and after several major battles, Jourdan and the other French forces retreated. By now Napoleon was making a name for himself, and while Jourdan was a great battlefield general, politics were of less interest to him. Even so, in 1804, with Napoleon now firmly in control of France, Jourdan was made a Marshal of France. The rest of the war saw him either in Italy or Spain trying to prop up Napoleon's brother Joseph.

By 1809, the British, under Arthur Wellesley (who would become the Duke of Wellington), were making successful inroads in Spain. Jourdan, as an acting advisor, was largely ignored by a new generation of generals who were losing to Wellington, and he was blamed for the defeats. After 1815, he accepted the Bourbon restoration and, in 1816, became the governor of Grenoble. In 1819, he was made a Peer of France. He wrote several books about his earlier campaigns and died in 1833, wealthy and respected by virtually everyone. Regarded as one of the most successful of the French Revolutionary commanders, Napoleon referred to him as a 'true patriot'.

11. 1795 SAW THE START OF A LEGEND

By 1795, France had been at war for years, and the situation in Paris was tumultuous. Rival political factions were itching for either more change or a return to the old ways. Throughout the year there had been skirmishes and confrontations between the republican National Convention and a royalist minority. The minority was relatively well armed, and there were even rumours that some of the Paris National Guard might defect to their cause.

Everything came to a bloody climax on 5 October when the National Convention came under attack by royalist forces; the capital itself was now under siege from the enemy within. It was at this point that Napoleon (who had been quietly climbing the ranks over recent years) took charge of the situation. He realised the best way to eradicate any threat on the streets of Paris was to set up artillery positions using cannon armed with grapeshot (this turned a cannon into a giant shot gun).

Napoleon was shrewd. He sensed the convention had little manoeuvring space and was utterly terrified. The daring twenty-six-year-old officer obtained permission for the troops to follow his orders – and it was then that he met Joachim Murat, who was to become one of his greatest and most loyal officers (Napoleon would eventually make him King of Naples). It was in the early morning of 5 October that Napoleon ordered Murat to bring him forty cannon. By dawn, Napoleon had managed to get all the cannon to high points or key crossroads to ensure a commanding advantage.

The royalists had managed to amass a formidable force of around 25,000, versus the 4,000 troops

Napoleon had at his disposal. However, the young officer was trained in artillery, and his positioning of the cannon was both pivotal and highly effective.

In the ensuing two-hour street battle, Napoleon's troops held firm, and between the musket volleys and the cannon blasting away, the royalists began to retreat. At this stage Napoleon ordered Murat to lead a cavalry charge against the retreating forces. He obliged, showing his verve and dynamism in carrying out the order.

This decisive defeat brought an end to the now shattered royalist resistance and made a national hero of Napoleon. The National Convention owed its very survival to this young officer who had acted so bravely and decisively (during the battle Napoleon's horse had been shot out from under him). How to reward such loyalty and ability? The answer was to give the man an army. And so Napoleon was installed as the General of the Army d'Italie.

When Napoleon reached his army near the Italian border in March of 1796, he found an ill-disciplined rabble, many without uniforms and some without shoes. It was short of supplies and ammunition, but it was an army, and the young general now had the tools to prove his ability.

12. The French Revolution Had an Impact on Ireland

One of the ideals of the French revolutionaries and, later, the National Convention, was to export republicanism to neighbouring states. This was completely understandable. After all, France wasn't the only nation with an autocratic ruler. But it is more than a little ironic that some of the earliest places to be attacked were the ones with more moderate governments. The Netherlands wasn't run by tyrants, nor was Britain, but Britain had long been a rival of France, and Britain had an Achilles' heel in Ireland.

For centuries, British rule in Ireland had been, at best mediocre, at times vague and at worst utterly heartless. The tensions within England's oldest colonial possession had long been evident and frequently exploded into full-blown rebellion. In the sixteenth century, the situation polarised as mainland Britain became largely Protestant, and Ireland remained staunchly Roman Catholic.

At first Spain, but later France, sought to support these Irish rebellions, often under the cover of helping their Catholic brethren. In reality, these were just ploys to exploit opportunities to work against the English, who had resisted all attempts of direct invasion.

Meanwhile, in Ireland, both the American Revolution and the French Revolution had not gone unnoticed. Both had overthrown their kings and won newfound freedoms for their citizens (neatly ignoring the tens of thousands executed during the French Reign of Terror, but no matter). So the Society of United Irishmen was born in the early 1790s. Its purpose was to fight for the kind of rights that the French and Americans had fought for – and won.

The French were only too obliging and, by 1796, had created a small fleet and an army of nearly 20,000 regular troops to help the society. It set sail, knowing it could be blasted out of the water if it met a squadron of warships from the Royal Navy. However, it wasn't the Royal Navy it needed to worry about but the weather. A gale blew up and the ships lurched onwards. The French invasion force actually made it to Bantry Bay in Ireland, where the United Irishmen could see the fleet agonisingly close to land. But the weather was so severe that no landing could be attempted; it was simply too dangerous. The fleet returned to Brest, battered and bedraggled. The journey had been for nothing.

For the Society of United Irishmen, this was a depressing setback, but it persevered. By 1798, over a quarter of a million Irishmen were members, but an organisation that large couldn't be kept secret. There was an uprising, but the British had been effective in stopping the flow of weapons to the society, and most of the leaders had been rounded up. The uprising was supported by only 1,000 French troops, and the attempted revolution suffered from poor equipment and a lack of leadership. In its frustration, the Catholic Society massacred some Protestant civilians in Wexford, so in this particular conflict, no one had the moral high ground.

13. There Were Many Little-Remembered Battles in Germany

1796 was to be a key year in the story of the French wars of this era. The National Convention at the time had, in essence, three armies. Two were sent into the Rhineland, and the third was meant to secure the borders with Italy. The two generals heading into southern Germany were Jean Victor Marie Moreau and the aforementioned Jourdan (Fact 10). Both were established and successful French generals, and as Belgium and the Netherlands had become largely peaceful, it was time to strike at some of France's longest-standing enemies: Austria and the southern German states.

The two French generals worked independently of each other. This was not a case of splitting forces in front of an enemy (usually a tactical disaster); these were two separate military units, which had the advantage of stopping the Austrians from concentrating their considerable military resources in just one area.

The first obstacle was crossing the Rhine itself, and both generals did so in a masterful display of manoeuvring. There followed many battles with the Austrians, all of which resulted in French victories. An example of one of these is the Battle of Altenkirchen, which has been largely forgotten even though both sides had significant troop numbers of around 20,000. Also, had the Austrians won, it would have stopped the French from crossing the Rhine, stifling the campaign before it had even begun. But across the huge number of engagements from 1792–1815, this battle had no famous personalities and was neither big enough nor important enough to survive being consigned to the appendices of history.

The real concern was that once again the French were on the offensive, and once again they were winning. However, the Austrians were led by the Archduke Charles (Fact 39), who had already met Jourdan at the Battle of Neerwinden and was proving himself to be a smart and flexible military tactician. The archduke allowed the French to continue their progress. He had positioned a weak screen of troops near Moreau to make sure Jourdan advanced cautiously while he (the archduke) brought the bulk of his troops towards Jourdan.

It was at the battles of Amberg and Wurzburg that the archduke reversed Jourdan's successes and forced him to retreat after two major defeats. This allowed Charles to concentrate his forces on Moreau. They met in October of that year at the Battle of Emmendingen, where the Austrians had a slightly smaller army. This battle was fought in the foothills of mountains, on the edges of forests and by the banks of the Elz River. The French fought bravely, but Charles used the terrain to his advantage, again employing manoeuvrability as a weapon in his arsenal.

Moreau suffered nearly 3,000 casualties and even lost some of his cannon. The Austrians had won, and the French beat a hasty retreat to their original borders. The Rhineland Campaign had been a complete failure and reminded Europe that Austria still had a formidable army.

14. NAPOLEON CONQUERED ITALY AND SHOCKED EUROPE

Things were looking up for Napoleon. He was the hero of Paris, he had an army and he was married to Josephine de Beauharnais (an older widow with two children). True, his army was a dishevelled, poorly equipped mob, but he believed he could turn it into a fighting force. Indeed, he wasted no time in doing so. He arrived to take charge in March of 1796, and just a month later, he was fighting the Battle of Montenotte against Austrians and Sardinians – and he won. Although this battle was much smaller than the engagements taking place in the Rhineland that same year, it proved that the Army d'Italie, in the right hands, could win.

Two very important factors were the keys to this campaign. Firstly, Napoleon kept his soldiers together. Even though they were initially a motley bunch, cohesion was vital. Armies often faced desertions, but while Napoleon was winning, he kept consolidating and pushing his troops into a foreign land. There must have been initial grumbles, but he galvanised this unpromising army into a fiercely efficient fighting machine. Speed was the second factor necessary to victory in this campaign. The list of Napoleon's battles won and towns captured came thick and fast. Although this meant that his troops didn't have much time to recover between engagements, it also meant that organising and co-ordinating efforts against them were impossible.

Next, and in the space of just one campaigning season, Napoleon launched a sensational blitz into the Italian peninsula. As the victories accumulated, the authorities back in France recognised that he was on a roll and gave him 50,000 reinforcements. This enabled Napoleon to consolidate his victories so that in the areas he had captured, any uprisings were brutally suppressed. As a result of the surrender of an entire country, the French Tricolour was adapted to create a new Italian flag, a version of which is still in use today.

The republican and atheist National Convention in France wanted Napoleon to remove the Pope, but Napoleon recognised this would create a power vacuum, resulting in even greater post-fighting instability, so he declined to do so. However, on other occasions, Napoleon wasn't shy about dismantling ancient regimes or religious organisations.

In one year Napoleon had managed to do what so many kings and emperors had failed to do: he had conquered Italy – and at the tender age of just twenty-seven. Flushed with success, he set aside a palace and called for his wife to join him. But while Napoleon was away on campaign, his blushing bride had her head turned by Hippolyte Charles, a dashing cavalry officer. Napoleon found out about the affair, and enormous pressure was put on Josephine to join her husband, the new hero of the revolution. He had conquered a country and provided a palace – and she still wouldn't come? Some women are just hard to please.

15. Brown Bess Built an Empire

The British Land Pattern Musket first went into service in 1722. This smoothbore, flintlock firearm became known as the 'Brown Bess' and was sold to countries as far afield as Sweden and Brazil. It would continue to be the British Army's main musket until 1838. This means that in conflicts such as the Seven Years' War, the American Revolution and the Napoleonic Wars the same basic type of musket was in use. The Brown Bess was the weapon of choice in some of the most important wars in world history.

The earlier, traditional musket had to be fired by pushing a musket ball, along with a charge of gunpowder and some wadding, with a ramrod down the barrel of the gun. It was painfully slow to reload, but so were all the muskets of the day. Well-trained soldiers could fire a shot about once every thirty seconds, but the smooth barrel made it very inaccurate, usually only effective to about 80 yards or so. This explains why soldiers lined up and fired volleys: all those projectiles flying off in vaguely the right direction are bound to hit something, in which case the effective range more than doubled to about 175 yards.

The Brown Bess was innovative in that everything required to fire the musket was all in one cartridge. The soldier took out a paper cartridge, tore the top off with his teeth (this was pre-health and safety days), poured the black powder and ball into the barrel, and then the cartridge itself was rammed down with the rod so as to keep everything tightly packed at the base of the barrel. Then, gunpowder was put onto a metal plate where the flintlock mechanism would come down. The flint would strike, causing a spark; the spark ignited the gunpowder in the 'pan'; the gunpowder travelled by means of a hole through to the barrel and the musket fired. Occasionally the gunpowder in the pan would fail to ignite the charge inside the barrel, so after an initial spark, nothing happened. All the noise with no actual firing was, of course, frustrating and was called 'a flash in the pan', a phrase still in use today.

Musket fire caused smoke to erupt from the barrel, which meant that with hundreds of men firing simultaneously, visibility quickly deteriorated on the battlefield. Even though the Brown Bess was an improvement on the earlier musket, all the priming and reloading meant that soldiers still fought most effectively in long, straight lines. The first line fired while the rows behind reloaded, a system that enabled relatively continuous fire by well-trained and disciplined troops.

When compared to a modern rifle, all of this sounds woefully inadequate. But in 1722, the Brown Bess was the cutting-edge musket of its day and, two generations later, had provided the standard way to load and prime a rifle in all armies.

16. FREDERICK WILLIAM III PERFORMED A TRICKY BALANCING ACT

France, Austria, Russia and, of course, Britain all had sizeable empires by the late eighteenth century. The one court that was a relative newcomer and very much a secondary military power was Prussia. Unlike the nations above, Prussia is the only one that doesn't exist anymore, and people are sometimes confused about where it was and what modern countries, or parts of them, made it up.

Prussia was a mixture of northern German lands and areas that are now part of Poland. It also included Königsberg, now known as Kaliningrad, located on the Baltic coast, which is, today, a tiny, entirely unattached part of Russia. At the time of the Napoleonic era, Prussia was a patchwork of ethnicities, languages and cultures, with a comparatively small but first-class army. A generation earlier, under Frederick the Great, Prussia had managed to fight Austria, Russia and France to a standstill.

That victory had come at a terrifying cost, and contrary to popular belief, Prussia was not a great warmongering state. In fact, the ruler in the late eighteenth century was the very cautious King Frederick William III. Prussia was part of the First Coalition; however, in 1795 after Frederick William got what he really wanted (the remaining independent areas of the Kingdom of Poland, which meant the end of Poland as a nation state from this time until the end of the First World War), he backed out of the coalition.

It had been a very clever diplomatic coup on the part of Prussia's king. With a minimum of fighting, he had added a large number of lands to his domain. He knew his country's recent history and wanted to avoid the devastation that Prussia had suffered under Frederick the Great, who had fought on bravely but at great cost to his people. It's also fair to say that Frederick William knew he was not in the same class of military leaders as his great uncle.

So for the next ten years, Frederick William did what he was undeniably very good at: diplomacy. He managed to keep Prussia out of the conflict until 1806, when France's continued belligerence gave him no choice but to fight. The conflict was a disaster for Prussia, which was crushed by Napoleon in just one campaign, and forced Frederick William and his family to flee to Russia.

Of course, this meant that when the tide turned against Napoleon, Frederick William now had very personal reasons to join the later coalitions against France. At this time Prussia was neither the biggest nor the most dominant fighting force in Europe, but the Prussian forces were well organised and well trained. In a list of battles after 1806, Prussia's army crops up at key moments on a surprisingly regular basis. After Napoleon was finally defeated, and it came to creating a new Europe at the Congress of Vienna, Frederick William had contributed enough to acquire further territorial gains for Prussia.

17. A Hero Was Born at the Battle of Cape St Vincent

There are a few giants of history who emerged in this period, real men who have passed from history into folklore and are now legends. The battle in 1797 at Cape St Vincent, off the coast of Portugal, heralded the arrival of one of these legendary figures.

The battle was sparked when a Spanish fleet (allied with France), sailing to link up with French forces escorting scores of Spanish merchant ships, ran into the Royal Navy's Mediterranean fleet, led by Admiral Jervis. Reporting to Jervis were two vice admirals and a rear admiral. However, it was one lower-ranked commodore, by the name of Horatio Nelson, who would capture the imagination.

In the navy, there is no such thing as a 'ship'. A frigate is different to a sloop and a schooner is different to a man-of-war – it can get very technical, very quickly. The key type of warship was a 'ship of the line'. It got its name because most naval engagements in this era involved lining up, side-by-side, with the enemy and blasting away with their broadside cannon. The size and number of cannon determined the rank of ships, which were then known as first, second or third rate (the phrase 'first rate', meaning 'the best', comes from these rankings). The reason for all this explanation is that in this particular engagement, the Royal Navy was not only outnumbered, it was also outgunned, but Jervis ordered an attack anyway.

The engagement started well, but the British ships drifted out of position, and the Spanish reacted faster than had been anticipated. This meant that the British couldn't get into position to cut off the Spanish unless the young commodore disobeyed one order by very loosely interpreting another. Nelson was determined to keep the Spanish in the fight (better to capture an enemy vessel than let it escape to fight another day). As a result, Nelson's ship, the *Captain*, came under simultaneous fire from six Spanish ships of the line, three of them with 112 guns each, and the Spanish flagship, armed with 130. Despite lethal fire, which destroyed most of his sails and much of the steering, Nelson brought the *Captain* alongside a Spanish ship and boarded her.

The Spanish ship, the *San Nicolás*, had lashed itself to another Spanish ship; Nelson was now forced to fight across two Spanish vessels, each one at least the same size as the *Captain*, or larger. Nelson cried, 'Westminster Abbey or Glorious Victory!' and with that, charged into the fray with his crew. Their attack was so ferocious that both ships quickly surrendered – a remarkable result considering Nelson's crew was outnumbered by at least two to one and had just survived an intense naval bombardment.

This was by no means the only engagement of the day, but it was the most daring and caught the imagination of the people back home. The Royal Navy had secured a key victory; the Spanish and French plans had been foiled and Nelson had become a hero.

18. CANNON HAD MULTIPLE USES

By the time of the Napoleonic Wars, cannon did a lot more than just fire cannon balls. Cannon balls were solid metal balls, often called round shot, of varying sizes but those used in land battles were rarely larger than a grown man's fist. However, propelled by gunpowder, they could travel miles and tear through timber, shatter medieval castle walls and rip through lines of troops. But these were not the only types of projectile that cannon of the nineteenth century could fire.

Major General Henry Shrapnel of the British artillery invented a time-delay fuse that detonated a cannon ball which sprayed smaller metal balls into ranks of troops. This greatly improved the cannon's effectiveness against infantry, and his name is the origin of the term 'shrapnel'.

Then there was the grapeshot or canister. This was a simpler version of the shrapnel bomb where a metal canister, filled with metal balls, effectively turned cannon into giant shot guns. At close quarters, a row of cannon firing canisters could shred even the bravest of cavalry charges.

Finally, for ship warfare, there was 'chain shot'. These were two cannon balls linked together by a metal chain. If fired into the rigging of an enemy vessel, it would destroy the sails and immobilise the ship, making it easier to board and capture.

So while modern hydraulic artillery had yet to be invented, by the nineteenth century, the art of cannon fire had already turned into a science.

19. India Forged a Military Celebrity

Much like Napoleon, another man who would cast a long shadow over virtually all the events of the Napoleonic Wars started the conflict in relative obscurity. In September of 1793, Arthur Wellesley had just purchased the rank of lieutenant colonel in the 33rd Regiment. This was not an unusual practice because, for over a century and for several generations to come, the primary way to secure a promotion was to buy it.

Along with the Duke of York (Fact 8), Wellesley was involved in the underwhelming and unsuccessful Netherlands campaign. In later life he said of these experiences, 'At least I learned what not to do, and that is always a valuable lesson.' A few years later, he went to seek his fame and fortune in India (in the hope of winning Catherine 'Kitty' Pakenham's father's consent to marry her), and it was here that he went from minor officer to something of a military celebrity.

Britain was, at this time, at war with Tipu Sultan, a man Napoleon was hoping to ally with purely to distract Britain from fighting in Europe. In 1798–99, the East India Company (with local Indian allies) had pushed into Tipu Sultan's territory of Mysore, a massive region of southern India, roughly the same size as England. It was during this campaign that Wellesley demonstrated his excellent skills in planning and logistics in an attempt to keep the rates of illness, which so often afflicted armies on the subcontinent, as low as possible.

It was also in India that Wellesley proved his bravery in multiple battles. Even when he came close to being wounded or killed, he remained cool under fire. The conflict in Mysore culminated in the siege of Seringapatam, where there was an artillery duel and attempts to storm the defences – both elements of siege craft were masterfully demonstrated by Wellesley. The bloody siege lasted a month and around 20 per cent of the defenders were killed, including, in the final assault, Tipu Sultan.

As the dust settled on the East India Company's new possession, Wellesley realised that India was very good for his career. He was appointed governor of the region and was further rewarded with a promotion to brigadier general in 1801. He would lead troops into battle again in the Second Anglo-Maratha War, which resulted in his overwhelming victory at Assaye. While there was to be a third and final Anglo-Maratha War after Wellesley left India, he was the leader who broke the back of one of the largest kingdoms on the sub-continent.

Arthur returned to Britain in 1805, by which time he was both rich and famous. He was able to marry Kitty in 1806, even though, on seeing her again after so long, he remarked, 'She has grown ugly, by Jove!' (Arthur was never known for his charm.) In a few years, Wellesley was to put all he had learned on a faraway continent to effective use in Europe.

20. Chivalry Ended in Malta

In 1798, Napoleon planned to strike a fatal blow to the British Empire. He had decided that the best way to do this was to capture Egypt and, from there, link up with Tipu Sultan in India. The plan was ambitious. Even with modern technology, this would have been a huge gamble, and in the late eighteenth century, it was nothing short of a dream. Yet the French government, in awe of Napoleon's achievements, signed off on it.

It was in transit that Napoleon's invasion force was most vulnerable, and his main concern was that his fleet might be intercepted by the Royal Navy. Vice Admiral Horatio Nelson (Fact 17) was, indeed, trying to track down the French fleet, but they kept just missing each other. However, it was the anxiety with which the French Navy kept looking over its shoulder for any sign of the British that led to an unintended consequence of the campaign.

In the summer of 1798, the French fleet arrived at Malta. By this time, Malta had been ruled by the Hospitaller Knights for over 250 years. These knights could trace their order back to the Middle Ages and the Crusades. In 1565, these knights had led an epic defence of the island against the full fury of the Ottoman Empire in its prime – and won. Their reputation across Europe was of nobility, chivalry and bravery.

When Napoleon asked permission for his fleet to dock and re-provision, he was told that only two ships at a time could do so. With Nelson on his way, this would have meant a long and dangerous delay. So, intending to speed things along, Napoleon attacked. The fighting lasted only a few hours, but the Hospitallers, who for nearly 700 years had fought and withstood the might of the likes of Saladin and Ottoman sultans, surrendered within days. Their leader, the marvellously named Grand Master Ferdinand von Hompesch zu Bolheim, meekly left the island and, a few weeks later, resigned his post, bringing to a close the martial side of an ancient organisation. It was an underwhelming end to an organisation long associated with bravery.

While Napoleon allowed the papacy to continue in Rome, he could not allow such an outmoded system of government to continue in this captured prize. (Later on, the Hospitallers did re-emerge as a purely charitable organisation; St John's Ambulance is an offshoot.) After installing a French governor, Napoleon replenished his fleet and headed off to Egypt.

The irony was that after an anachronistic government had lasted for so long, the more modern French style of rule lasted only two years. One deeply unpopular French policy was the attempt to eradicate Roman Catholicism, which completely failed to take into account the fact that the small island had as many Catholic churches as days of the year. The Maltese people rebelled and asked the British for help. After Nelson imposed a blockade of the island, the French surrendered, and Malta voluntarily became a British Dominion.

21. THE PYRAMIDS WITNESSED NAPOLEON'S ARRIVAL IN THE MIDDLE EAST

Napoleon and his invasion fleet arrived in Egypt without further incident and landed safely at Alexandria. The choice was deliberate. While the Alexandria of 1798 was a tiny city in decline, it was a well-known name in the West; Napoleon's reputation would be further enhanced when it was learned that his first act in Egypt was to capture such an ancient and famous city.

When they disembarked, the French faced a further hangover from the era of the Crusades: the Mamelukes. They had originally been a slave army but had risen to power in the thirteenth century. By the late eighteenth century, they were, in theory, under Ottoman rule but were, in fact, semi-autonomous. Their cavalry was the stuff of legends. It was an elite force which had beaten the Mongols in their prime and had been the most feared mounted force at the Ottoman sultans' disposal. Before the French could conquer Egypt, they would have to face these warriors and beat them in their own territory.

While European armies wore bright colours to stand out on the battlefield, the Mamelukes took uniforms to a whole new level: their jackets were made of yellow and green silk; plumes from exotic birds adorned their brightly coloured turbans and their scimitars were embossed with ivory or silver. They were the epitome of exotic – and they were deadly.

The French may have looked less ostentatious, but Napoleon's troops were well-trained and battle-hardened. Napoleon met the Mamelukes near the pyramids, another location steeped in history. Forced to fight against an alien enemy in the July heat of Egypt,

Napoleon rallied his troops: 'Forward! Remember that from those monuments yonder forty centuries look down upon you!'

The French infantry assumed the anti-cavalry formation of a hollow square. The Mamelukes threw themselves at these formations, not only demonstrating their bravery but also showing how outmoded their tactics were. Napoleon had chosen a location that split his enemy's forces. While on paper the two armies were of roughly equal size, a significant number of local troops and cavalry were on the wrong side of the Nile. The fact that they were unable to cross and engage in a timely manner meant that the French actually had superior numbers; they also had better tactics and more modern weaponry.

The French held firm, and Napoleon ordered an attack on the nearby town and Mameluke stronghold of Embabeh. It was quickly captured, and the Mamelukes were pushed back by volley after volley of musket fire. The fighting turned into a rout as the Mamelukes broke off and fled; many were forced into a river where hundreds drowned.

By the end of the day, the Mamelukes had lost around 3,000 men, whereas the French recorded just twenty-nine dead. While it was not quite the end of the Mamelukes, it was their most humiliating defeat for centuries. Napoleon had announced his arrival in the Middle East.

22. The Battle of the Nile Wasn't Fought on the Nile

Napoleon always had his eye on the newspapers back home. This was evident with his decision to land at Alexandria, and the same was true of the Battle of the Nile, which actually took place just off the coast of Egypt in Aboukir Bay – but that just doesn't have the same ring to it.

Two weeks after Napoleon's devastating defeat of the Mamelukes, the Royal Navy finally caught up with the French fleet, harbouring in the relative safety of the Egyptian bay. Each force was roughly the same size, and each had thirteen ships of the line. The French also had their flagship *L'Orient*, a massive warship with 120 guns (of varying size) and over 1,000 crew and marines on board. By comparison, Rear Admiral Nelson's flagship was the HMS *Vanguard* with seventy-five guns.

Although the French were anchored, the French Admiral François-Paul Brueys d'Aigalliers (generally referred to as Brueys, for the sake of brevity) assumed that he was close enough to shore to ensure his line of ships could act as a defensive wall against any attack by the British.

Once again, Nelson showed flair, tactical ability and bravery. And, unusually, he trusted that, if in the heat of battle following orders to the letter was not possible, his officers would follow the 'spirit' of his orders.

Brueys was half right in his calculation that his ships were safely positioned. As they attempted to get behind the French line, several British ships hit rocks and floundered, but in the initial attack, five warships were able to slip behind the French, who now faced close-quarter cannon fire from two sides.

The Royal Navy blasted away, splintering the French ships, and the ones facing fire from two sides surrendered. Meanwhile, even as *L'Orient* turned one British vessel into a floating wreck, the fighting focussed on the French flagship. The artillery duels were fierce, and the battle continued on into the night. Brueys was struck by a cannon ball, which severed both his legs. Undaunted, he ordered his men to prop him up in a barrel where he continued to give orders as he slowly died of his wounds.

When fire broke out on *L'Orient*, the store of gunpowder caught fire and detonated. The explosion was so severe and the shock waves so enormous that all fighting stopped. Even though both sides pulled many from the water, only around 100 men survived. The rest of the French fleet surrendered. It had been a bloody but decisive British victory.

The fighting had been so brutal that Nelson, too, was severely wounded, and it was thought he would die. Some sailors actually cut away part of *L'Orient*'s main mast to use as his coffin, but he survived. With the loss of his fleet, Napoleon's plan to use Egypt as a launch pad to attack India was over.

23. Napoleon Toured the Middle East

In 1799, Napoleon faced the unsavoury prospect of being trapped in Egypt. The locals were starting to rise up against French rule, and he was cut off from effective resupply because the Royal Navy was positioned just off the coast; Napoleon dropped all of his earlier plans and decided to attack Palestine, another Ottoman territory.

He arrived, in March, at the medieval walled city of Jaffa, a major centre for trade and garrison to elite Ottoman troops. If this campaign was to be successful, if he wanted to go any further, Napoleon had to take the city. After besieging the walls and threatening a breach, Napoleon sent a Turkish emissary to discuss terms of surrender. The city's commander had him beheaded. Napoleon retorted with a furious and efficient assault in which he quickly captured the city. While the capture was done with his usual efficiency, he rather uncharacteristically ordered a massacre. It was so extensive and so ruthless that in order to save ammunition, he ordered some of the prisoners to be bayoneted or drowned. He did allow some to leave the city, hoping they would spread fear; instead, their reports stiffened resistance.

Napoleon continued his march north and took a number of other key cities until, finally, he came to city of Acre. Acre had been the last European crusader city in the Middle East, but it had fallen in 1291. Now, for the first time in over 500 years, a western army was once again near. But times had changed, and the Ottomans were now working in conjunction with the Royal Navy to stop Napoleon's continuing advance up the eastern Mediterranean coast. The two opposition leaders were Jezzar Pasha (obviously a local) and Sidney Smith (obviously not a local). It was Smith who positioned his ships so as to prevent any chance of a French naval resupply, with the added advantage that they were close enough to shore to fire on the French attackers.

The combination of fierce resistance by the locals, along with the modern artillery of the Royal Navy, meant that Napoleon, having lost about 20 per cent of his force in a two-month siege, had no choice but to call off the campaign and head back to Egypt. Some of his troops had caught plague, and he ordered them to be poisoned so as not to be captured by the Ottomans, who were sure to torture them. Even so, this was another low point in Napoleon's campaign.

Napoleon had reached his limits in the Middle East and now had to look elsewhere for victory. A few months later, he managed to set sail back to France, leaving virtually his entire army in Egypt to 'administer' it. The reality was that he deserted his forces, leaving them to fight a growing rebellion, with no hope of reinforcements. Massacre, poisoning, desertion: 1799 was one of Napoleon's most ignoble years. Napoleon knew this and blamed Smith, saying, '[He] robbed me of my destiny.'

24. The Second Coalition Was Meant to Be the Last One

Napoleon's move towards Egypt triggered a second phase of diplomatic activity in an attempt to raise some kind of alliance against France in general and against Napoleon in particular. Because Napoleon had yet to become the overall ruler, both the First and Second Coalitions were created to counter revolutionary France. This Second Coalition would last from 1798–1802.

While Napoleon was busy fighting in Egypt, General Jourdan was, once again, advancing against the Austrians ... who turned to a new ally: Russia. Russia, at this time, was a minor partner, as mustering and sending troops from far away Moscow would simply take too long, but the potential of a country with the resources of Russia was huge. Britain was part of the coalition, but it was Napoleon's actions that brought fresh players into this war. While Napoleon could rely on new forces from the recently conquered Italy, his actions further south had provoked the Ottoman Empire, which had been attacked in Egypt and, later, Palestine, and which looked to the West for assistance against the belligerent French general now in Ottoman lands.

Denmark flirted with joining the French, but as Britain feared the Baltic would become hostile to British shipping, Nelson fought the Battle of Copenhagen and convinced the Danes to stay out of the war. In a complex situation, this unprovoked conflict meant that Britain had attacked a neutral country.

Peace treaties were signed in 1802, bringing an end to the Second Coalition. For a brief period, peace reigned.

25. A Stone Revealed the Secrets of Ancient Egypt

When Napoleon arrived with his invasion force in Egypt, he didn't just bring soldiers, he also brought nearly 200 scientists. Thanks to this bizarre addition to a military campaign, Napoleon can be credited with enabling the many archaeological and other finds that resulted, but none was more important than a soldier's discovery of a curious stone in a wall.

The stone, which was being used simply as building material in an old and unexceptional wall, was large and black, with very exotic looking inscriptions. It was found near the town of Rosetta and has become known as the Rosetta Stone. The importance of the stone is that it has the same inscription carved in three different languages: Ancient Greek, Demotic and Egyptian Hieroglyphs. However, almost as soon as the French had discovered this remarkable object, they lost it. This was because the Royal Navy combined with a local rebellion to thwart the French invasion. To the victors belong the spoils, so the stone (which was then deemed to be of little importance to the Egyptians; they had far grander monuments from their ancient past) became British property and was presented to the British Museum in 1802.

The granodiorite stone itself is of no commercial value; it's the inscriptions that are the real treasure. Even in the Napoleonic era the Ancient Egyptian civilisation was well known in the West, not least because it is mentioned extensively in the Old Testament, but, except for the translation of a few royal names, nothing much was known about the language. However, the ability to cross reference the two known languages with the unknown hieroglyphs meant that the code of this long-dead language was cracked, even to the extent that pronunciations could be guessed. It was eventually determined that the stone had come originally from a temple or from near a temple. It had been carved in the different language inscriptions due to the fact that after Alexander the Great had conquered Egypt, the Egyptian royal family was then, at least partly, Greek, with strong connections to Greek cities.

The work of deciphering the stone went on for a generation, and it wasn't until the 1820s that accurate translations were revealed for the first time. As the stone gave up its secrets, the records revealed all aspects of Egyptian life, from the grand decrees of the pharaohs, to information about the world's first recorded labour dispute and strike (it happened in 1152 BC over pay; the labourers eventually got a wage increase). Slightly more worrying for the Church, the translated Egyptian records showed a rather different version of Old Testament events than that of the traditional Jewish version. The Biblical texts had always been presumed to be ... well, Gospel.

This serendipitous find can be traced back to a soldier under the command of a French general, who enabled science to unlock the lives of those in one of the most ancient civilisations in the world.

26. A MEAL WAS NAMED AFTER A BATTLE

By late 1799, Napoleon was back in Europe and had wrangled his way to the top of the pile in revolutionary France. However, he knew full well that all his achievements could easily be undone if he didn't keep winning. So, in the spring of 1800, he crossed the Alps to take on an Austrian invasion of northern Italy.

There is a famous picture, by Jacques-Louis David, of Napoleon crossing the Alps on horseback. It's one of the definitive images of Napoleon, all flowing robes and dashing machismo. It is, however, pure propaganda. We know that Napoleon used a donkey, rather than a horse, and as the weather was terrible, everyone was bundled in as many layers as they could find. The truth is that Napoleon would have looked something like a vagrant on a mangy mount, rather than the image in the painting – but then again, Napoleon wasn't always big on the truth.

Even in the atrocious conditions of an alpine crossing, Napoleon demonstrated the speed at which he could move an army. He quickly seized a number of towns and cities before the Austrians could react. Eventually, he met the Austrians at Marengo. By now Napoleon had an army of around 25,000, against an army about a third again as big as his.

The action took place in the valley of the Bormida River, which was a key feature in the battle as traversing any lake or bridge can cause bottlenecks or issues of manoeuvre. The Austrians attacked first, and the French absorbed the initial clash. After hours of fighting, the battle was beginning to slow to a bloody deadlock.

By mid-afternoon, however, the weight of the

Austrian forces was starting to take its toll, and the French were pushed back. An attempt to envelop and surround the French flank was halted by General Kellerman, whose heavy cavalry stabilised the French and allowed an orderly retreat to new positions. This manoeuvre spread the Austrians thinly, and it was at this stage that Napoleon started a counter-attack.

Kellerman and a General Desaix charged all of the French cavalry on the flanks of the Austrian army and shattered it. In the fierce fighting, some of the Austrian ammunition was set alight, causing further noise and confusion. The Austrians lost more than 10,000 men and a good proportion of their cannon. The result was significant, but a calm reading of the battle suggests that things went the way of the Austrians for most of the day and that it was only a final, perfectly timed counterattack that prevented a French defeat. It was an important victory because it stopped further Austrian invasions of Italy and reinforced Napoleon's formidable reputation.

Chicken Marengo is a dish named after this clash. Legend says that it was served to Napoleon after the battle, but this is unlikely. A more probable explanation is that a local chef created it to commemorate Napoleon's victory.

27. THE ROYAL NAVY ATTACKED A CITY

As briefly mentioned in Fact 24, Britain attacked a neutral country for fear of it becoming a French ally. In this respect, the Battle of Copenhagen, in 1801, was lamentable. However, with Napoleon absconding from the Middle East in 1799, and then spectacularly humbling Austria at Marengo, the whole of Europe was panicking over what would happen next. Denmark and Norway were being courted by France, and if they could be persuaded to join the fight, Russia might also join them. The possibility that Denmark might attack the British mainland could not be contemplated. Something had to be done.

Step forward Admiral Parker, who was sent to carry out some very British gunboat diplomacy – i.e. turn up with some warships and force a settlement. It wasn't necessarily meant to be a shooting war. When the Royal Navy arrived, the Danish fleet was moored against the gun batteries and naval defences of the city, so a frontal assault would have been insane.

However, Parker's subordinate was Vice Admiral Nelson, who was just the right mix of brilliant, brave and insane. He attacked the weaker southern end of the Danish defences, which resulted in a brutal artillery duel between land and sea. Parker lacked Nelson's grit and, on seeing the devastating effect of close-quarter cannon fire, signalled the retreat. Nelson replied with a signal that acknowledged the order – but did nothing. Instead, he lifted his telescope to his blind eye and said to his captain (Thomas Foley), 'You know, Foley, I only have one eye. I have the right to be blind sometimes.' With that, he continued to press his attack. In the heat of the battle, he was seen to be carefully preparing a letter for the terms of Copenhagen's surrender. It is not surprising that his attention to such matters, amid the roar of cannon, the screams of men and the sound of splintering wood, forced at least one of his officers to conclude that Nelson had lost his mind, but Nelson calmly explained that if he was seen to have the time and the conditions to prepare a decent letter, it would make the Danes think they weren't causing as much damage as they were. It was remarkable logic and shows the ultimate cool head under fire.

The ruse worked and Copenhagen surrendered. Remarkably, no Royal Navy ships were sunk; however, 1,200 British crew were either killed or wounded. The Danes suffered 50 per cent more casualties and lost three ships, including their flagship, the *Dannebrog*, when it exploded.

After this short but bloody encounter, the two nations agreed an armistice. Following this, Parker sailed the fleet to Sweden in an attempt to persuade it to break away from the armed neutrality league that had been set up in the Baltic, but the Swedes declined his offer. As a result of Parker's wavering at Copenhagen, followed by his rather lacklustre display in Sweden, he was relieved of duty, and Nelson was promoted to admiral.

Charles Maurice de Talleyrand-Périgord, known to history simply as Talleyrand, was a diplomat and a key figure, not only throughout the years of these wars but also both before and after. Not bad for a man who started out as an ordained priest.

The French Revolution (like many revolutions) never completely wiped the slate clean. Skill gaps aren't just a modern phenomenon, and most rebels come to understand that they need the expertise of old hands. In the case of Talleyrand, he had already risen to Bishop of Autun and was the Roman Catholic Church's representative to the court of Louis XVI. Being both a member of the clergy and a member of the French king's court should have been enough to have his head removed in the bloodier stages of the French Revolution. However, he dodged the executioner by supporting the appropriation of church lands and was later sent as an ambassador to Britain to avert war. He excelled in both of these roles, which enabled him to keep his head and gave him the credentials to continue his career.

In 1799, he was instrumental in helping with Napoleon's move to become the First Consul, thus allying himself to the right side of that power struggle. He became Napoleon's Chief Foreign Advisor and, later, his Minister of Foreign Affairs for most of the rest of the war. In 1801, in a highly unusual move, the Pope 'laicised' Talleyrand (turned him from a bishop back into a layman).

Tallyrand was a controversial figure who had an uneasy relationship with Napoleon. He usually delivered what Napoleon wanted, but this was not always what Talleyrand thought was best. Napoleon wallowed in victory and enjoyed rubbing the noses of the nations he had defeated in their subjugation. Talleyrand, by contrast, was more of a liberal and a visionary who wanted a nobler outcome for peace treaties, pointing out (correctly) that punitive peace agreements usually led to resentment and increased the chances of further war in the long term. Talleyrand also recognised that Napoleon wouldn't keep winning indefinitely and that France didn't have the resources to constantly fight all of the rest of Europe.

Because he both served and survived the major French regimes of his time, he is seen by some as a traitor and, by others, as a skilled diplomat. He was regarded, throughout Europe, as a genius when it came to understanding foreign affairs. When his rift with Napoleon became too great, he resigned his posts in 1807. In 1814, he was the chief French negotiator for peace and a key player in the restoration of the French monarchy.

Talleyrand had a remarkable career which spanned many different governments and endured through peace, revolution and war. He retired in 1815 but returned to active service at the request of the new French King Louis-Philippe, who appointed him French ambassador to Britain from 1830–34. Following this, he retired again and enjoyed a few years of well-deserved ease before his death in 1838.

29. Nelson Had an Unusual Private Life

Horatio Nelson was a hero in his own lifetime, and he knew it. After the Battle of the Nile, there were spontaneous celebrations wherever he went. He received gifts from the Russian and Ottoman courts and, of course, was lavished with gifts and titles in Britain too.

On his return from Egypt, he stopped at Naples for repairs and resupply. It was here that he met Sir William and Emma Hamilton, and while they all enjoyed themselves at a seemingly endless number of balls, banquets and entertainments, he and Emma became lovers.

You might think that this would have led to 'pistols at dawn' between Sir William and Nelson, but you'd be wrong. Naturally, the navy kept Nelson at sea for most of the time, but in 1801, when he returned to England, he moved in with both of the Hamiltons. It seems that Sir William, who was more than thirty years older than Emma, was happy to host such a hero and keep him ... let's use the term 'entertained'. So entertained was Nelson that in 1801, Emma gave birth to his only child, a daughter called Horatia.

In 1802, Nelson bought Merton Place in Surrey, and all three moved there together. William died in 1803, and shortly after, Nelson sailed off on what was to be his last campaign, leaving behind the two women in his life. Emma would later become the muse of the painter George Romney, while Horatia married a curate and had ten children.

30. THE 'SEA WOLF' WAS NOT ADMIRAL NELSON

Throughout this period the most powerful force Britain had was not its army but its navy, and while Nelson took many of the headlines, he was not the only remarkable officer in the Royal Navy. Perhaps the most unorthodox, challenging even Nelson for the title of 'bravest sailor,' was a largely forgotten naval officer by the name of Thomas Cochrane.

This tall and imposing Scot faced a court martial over flippancy and, in 1814, was mired in a stock market scandal (he was later exonerated). However, it was with his sloop (small warship) HMS *Speedy* that he caused all kinds of damage around the Spanish coast. He was so good at pouncing on lone ships that Napoleon nicknamed him the 'Sea Wolf'. Cochrane was the inspiration for C. S. Forester's Horatio Hornblower and Patrick O'Brian's Jack Aubrey novels; the latter novels were the basis for the film *Master and Commander: The Far Side of the World*.

An engagement that illustrates his bravery and skill occurred in 1801, when he approached a Spanish warship (*El Gamo*) with six times as many men and more than double the number of guns that Cochrane had. By flying the American flag (a neutral country at the time), he tricked the Spaniards into getting close enough to board. As he neared, he fired all his guns but made sure he was so close that the *El Gamo* couldn't return fire (the Spanish guns couldn't aim far enough down to hit the much smaller vessel). Consequently, he faced being swamped by Spanish sailors and marines and had to break away, but not so far as to be obliterated by the Spanish guns. However, it was just far enough away to fire another broadside before moving up to *El Gamo*'s side again.

This careful manoeuvring went back and forth three times before Cochrane and all but one of his crew boarded the much larger vessel, leaving just the ship's doctor behind. During the fighting, Cochrane bellowed to the doctor to send the reinforcements, and the doctor, replying that he would, fooled the Spanish into thinking there were far more sailors on the *Speedy* than there were. At around the same time, one of Cochrane's officers took down the Spanish flag (colours), which was usually a sign of surrender; and in all the confusion, the Spanish did surrender.

Cochrane brought the Spanish warship to Minorca (a British-held island); it was a prize that dwarfed his own ship. Cochrane's unique attitude meant he was always at odds with the Royal Navy's command. After serving for twenty years, he resigned and went on to become a valuable asset to other navies. He ended up in South America where he was a leading officer in the Chilean and Brazilian navies. He even helped the Greeks in their war of independence against the Ottoman Empire. However, as forgotten as he is in Britain, every year on Chile's Independence Day, a delegation of naval officers lays a wreath on his tomb in Westminster Abbey.

31. NAPOLEON TOOK CHARGE ... OF FRANCE

When Napoleon returned to Paris from Egypt in 1799, he was not in a good mood. Josephine was not waiting for him, which angered him so much that he threatened divorce. His mood wasn't helped by the fact that France had descended into such poor governance that his baggage had been stolen.

France was suffering on a grand scale. The revolutionary government was both incompetent and corrupt, and hyper-inflation was destroying the economy. Napoleon believed he was the man to take charge and enlisted the help of his political ally Sieyès (a revolutionary theorist), Talleyrand and his brother Lucien.

Napoleon lied to the Council of 500 about a Jacobin plot ... which allowed him to deliver his own *coup d'état* and seize power, bringing the Directory (the second half of the revolution) to an end. It helped that he had the only troops in the area, so while not a shot was fired, the implied force was there. Napoleon proved to be as adept at political manoeuvres as military ones when he established the French Consulate, a triumvirate of rulers, but one that did not include Sieyès because of their constitutional differences. (Brother Lucien later went into self-imposed exile because of disagreements with his brother.)

While, theoretically, three men now ruled France, in reality, there was only one with real power: Napoleon. In the space of four years he had gone from obscurity, to notoriety as the most feared general in Europe, to the de facto ruler of France.

32. WILLIAM PITT WAS A VERY YOUNG PRIME MINISTER

William Pitt was a British Prime Minister in the mid-eighteenth century; his second son became Prime Minister in 1783, and he was also called William ... so he became known as William Pitt the Younger, an apt title because he was then just twenty-four.

Pitt had become a Member of Parliament two years earlier by running in a 'rotten borough' (a constituency with a small electoral population, usually under the control of a local land owner). This was the start of what should have been a career steeped in corruption and naked political ambition, and while there were undoubtedly elements of the latter, it's ironic that Pitt later tried to do away with the rotten boroughs.

Pitt was the British Prime Minister for seventeen years, including the period that covered the outbreak of war with France and Napoleon's rise to power. In 1788, George III fell ill, and his self-indulgent son was appointed Prince Regent. What was worse for Pitt was that the heir to the throne was a supporter of Pitt's main challenger, Charles Fox. While Pitt chose to put the good of the country and the government above his own career, he also knew something about political manoeuvring and managed to remain in power.

It was Pitt's government that was the driving force behind the formation of the two coalitions that opposed French military aggression, and it was Pitt's policy to get as many nations as possible to try and contain France and her expansionist plans. Because he was a skilled politician, Pitt managed to pull natural enemies together to fight a power that had clear military supremacy in Europe.

Wars are expensive and Pitt was the first to come up with a novel new tax: income tax, something that we are all too familiar with today. Even so, Pitt was forced to double the national debt, but he was prudent in its financing. It was also Pitt who took the decision to substitute paper bank notes for gold. Although it was not planned, he understood that this was the way to stop a run on the gold reserves, and in the process, he changed a traditional economy into a modern one.

However, in 1801, when King George III was enjoying a lucid period, Pitt and the king fell out over Catholic emancipation in Ireland. Pitt was for and George was against. Pitt resigned but returned in 1804 to head up the Houses of Parliament. Napoleon was then at the peak of his powers, but while Pitt did all he could to work for containment, he felt overwhelmed by the situation.

Pitt had never been a healthy man, and his one major vice was alcohol. Although instructed to drink wine for medicinal reasons, his real taste seems to have been for port. This may well have been the cause of his death in 1806 (one of the few Prime Ministers to die in office). He was then only forty-six, but had spent nearly twenty years as British Prime Minister.

33. THERE WAS A REVOLUTION AGAINST REVOLUTIONARY FRANCE

The impact of the French revolutionary wars rippled out to many unexpected shores. Napoleon in Egypt is a well-known example, but another, less well-known case comes from the French Caribbean colony of Saint Domingue. This colony was a huge cash cow thanks to its enormous exports of coffee and sugar, worth a fortune in Europe. The colony was simply too important to lose.

It's ironic that the ideals of the French Revolution, which, in theory, were about freedom and equality, didn't extend to the black slaves in the Caribbean. The white French colonial landowners thought the revolution would allow them more freedom and that they would be able to rule their plantations pretty much as they saw fit. The slaves sensed that their atrocious conditions could get even worse.

What started in 1791 as a breakaway from the motherland for financial gain, turned into a full-blown slave revolt. Its leader was the self-educated, free black man Toussaint L'Ouverture, who became known as the 'Black Napoleon'. He was an improbable trailblazer who had mastered the art of guerrilla warfare and then led a regular army to dominate the territory, defeating both French and, later, Spanish forces. As the leader of the newly independent country of Haiti, inspired by enlightenment ideals, L'Ouverture created a new constitution and a new economy; he even entered into trade negotiations (and therefore achieved international recognition) with the United States and Britain.

However, in 1801, Napoleon sent a fleet with troops

to take back both the French- and Spanish-held areas of the island. They did so with relative ease and not much fighting. L'Ouverture was promised that the changes he had made would be honoured if he stepped down. He agreed but was betrayed and was shipped back to France where he died in prison.

For his next move, Napoleon, that great egalitarian, tried to reintroduce slavery in the Spanish areas of the island, and so the revolution erupted again under L'Ouverture's right-hand man, Jean-Jacques Dessaline, who finished what L'Ouverture had started. The French troops were expelled, and the Republic of Haiti was established in 1804. Almost immediately after the French forces had left, Dessaline ordered the massacre of white plantation owners, effectively wiping out the white Haitian population of 3,000–5,000. Maybe it is Dessaline who should be remembered as the 'Black Napoleon' because, as soon as the republic was established, he declared himself emperor. He was ambushed in 1806, when he was (depending on which account you prefer) either shot or stabbed or, possibly, both. He leaves a complex legacy in Haiti, not only as the father of independence but also as a blood-thirsty tyrant.

The Haitian slave revolt is the only one to have led to the founding of a country, the first independent state in the Americas. The events that led to this revolution took place on another continent an ocean away, and yet its repercussions were to affect slave-trading countries throughout the western world.

34. THE 'DEFINITIVE TREATY OF PEACE' WAS NOT DEFINITIVE

By 1801, Napoleon was casting around for a peace deal. With the debacle in Egypt behind him, he was once more on a winning streak, his European victories humbling both the Austrians and the Russians. While not an all-conquering hero, Napoleon could negotiate from a position of strength and gain favourable terms for France at a time when the country had had little respite from war and civil turmoil for more than a decade. France needed time to regroup and recuperate.

The mainland European powers had already sued for peace; it was only Britain that remained at war with France. The two powers could both claim their greatest number of successes in the last few years of fighting, and so the Treaty of Amiens, created by two equal powers, was designed to establish a 'Definitive Treaty of Peace'. Had the fighting ended here, we could, with hindsight, say that Napoleon would have missed out on some of his greatest victories, but at the same time, he also would have been saved from his biggest mistakes. In 1801, Napoleon was seen as an excellent general who was trying to restore order to an exhausted, corrupt and politically turbulent France. Putting it simply, he was a man Britain believed it could do business with.

The treaty was one of those classic eighteenth- and nineteenth-century documents that carved up territories as if they were pawns in a board game. The British negotiator was Charles Cornwallis (the one who surrendered to the American and French forces at Yorktown), while the French relied on Talleyrand. It was their intention to write a treaty that would create peace for future generations. The examples below show not only the level of mutual respect but also the breadth of areas being discussed:

France was to give Britain Trinidad (in the Caribbean) and Ceylon (in Asia).

Britain was to withdraw from Egypt.

Britain was to return the Cape Colony (South Africa) to the Batavian Republic (basically the Netherlands, a French ally).

In this one document countries separated by vast oceans and continents were being traded like tokens. In an interesting addendum, it was specifically noted that the fact that the treaty was in French and English was not meant to be an insult to the other nations involved.

While Napoleon was determined to keep Britain out of continental European affairs, he just couldn't do the same and sent military forces to intervene in small territories like the Cisalpine Republic. Equally, Britain did not carry out all that it had promised either (i.e. the evacuation of Malta – it was just too strategic a naval base). Also, just before war had formally broken out, all French merchant shipping then in Britain had been confiscated. Exactly who was the worst offender of the treaty's terms depends on your point of view, but it's fair to say that the British government didn't want another war, whereas Napoleon did.

About a year after peace was agreed, war was declared.

35. Another Coalition Was Created: Round Three

After the brief peace, war drums sounded again in 1803. France and Britain were the first two to clash, and by now a pattern was emerging. Britain didn't have the kind of army that could counter Napoleon's forces on the continent, but at the same time, despite the French and Spanish navies being technically formidable on paper, they were constantly being beaten by the Royal Navy. In order to prevent a military deadlock, Britain looked around for allies.

At first glance, the lists of those aligned against France throughout the late eighteenth and early nineteenth centuries seem to be similar (hint: Britain and Austria always fight on the same side), with other powers coming and going, depending on Napoleon's current targets. Because of Napoleon's attacks on Egypt and Palestine, the Second Coalition had included the Ottoman Empire; however, after that France never again threatened Ottoman lands, so that empire did not join any further coalitions.

Napoleon's actions at this time were so extreme that Britain didn't need to look far for allies. The first to join the Third Coalition (1803–06) were the Swedes, who feared their more southerly possessions might be attacked by France. And Napoleon certainly didn't help himself when, in 1804, he had Louis Antoine de Bourbon tried (on very weak evidence) and executed for plotting his assassination. While the death penalty was then not uncommon in any country in Europe, this execution was seen as politically motivated. Killing a junior member of the old French dynasty brought back memories of The Terror, when thousands of aristocrats were murdered.

Talleyrand was doing his best to ensure that France didn't isolate itself because of the behaviour of its First Consul (Napoleon), who was deliberately antagonistic to the other major European powers. By contrast, William Pitt the Younger recognised that the hand Napoleon had dealt him would guarantee further alliances for the British, who yet again provided the backbone to an anti-French coalition.

Spain was, once again, supporting France (along with French-run areas of Italy), and once again, the Russians and the Holy Roman Empire of the Austrians would oppose them. The stakes had been high during the Second Coalition, but this time they were even higher. In 1804, no one knew that the coming era would see Napoleon at the peak of his powers and that it would be an era that would change the political map of Europe forever. It was during this time that Britain would face the threat of invasion, the most serious since the era of the Spanish Armada over 200 years earlier.

The next few facts will deal with some of the most dramatic events of this period, one of which would see the destruction of the Holy Roman Empire. This conglomeration of German-speaking territories had played a key role in European politics since the late tenth century, and while it was well past its prime, no one could help but be impressed by its list of emperors going back over eight centuries.

36. A General Became an Emperor

The conspiracy to kill Napoleon, allegedly led by Louis Antoine de Bourbon, gave Napoleon an excuse to raise the matter of that primary anathema of revolutionary values: hereditary monarchy ... specifically and paradoxically, Napoleon's intention to be the new hereditary monarch.

Napoleon ensured that the constitution was changed so that any return to hereditary rule would go to him and his bloodline, not to the old (and still living) Bourbon family. The provisions were formally ratified, although it should be noted that it was not advisable to vote against Napoleon's wishes. But it was all for the best – and definitely in France's best interests.

More than 4,000 people came to see the coronation of Napoleon, some having arrived the day before so they could witness this historic moment. Napoleon wore a long white satin tunic embroidered with gold, as did Josephine, for she was to be crowned too. It's a little ironic that the man who had come to power in an anti-monarchy revolution and who was to abolish the oldest existing imperial title in Europe (the Holy Roman Emperor) only shortly after this, would create a new imperial title. He did this, so he said, because he did not want to be seen as having been descended from the Bourbons, but in reality, by 1804, Napoleon could do pretty much as he wished. Why not become an emperor rather than a king?

The ceremony was bursting with the symbols of the old regime. The coronation was in Notre Dame Cathedral where two full orchestras and four choirs played him into his new role. Pope Pius VII was there to anoint them both with chrism, an essential ritual in which an ordinary man could become acceptable as an emperor in the eyes of God ... all this for a man who claimed to be an atheist. In fact, for a secular, atheist anti-monarchist, this was about as extreme a U-turn as could be imagined. And it was not over yet. In a final moment of ego, just as the Pope was about to lay the golden laurel wreath on his head, Napoleon grabbed it and crowned himself. This story is challenged; some believe it to be apocryphal, but others think it fits Napoleon's belief that he did not depend on anyone for his authority.

In his oath, he swore to protect the French Republic, which was a further irony, given the circumstances. And just for good measure, in 1805, having got the hang of being a monarch, he crowned himself King of Italy.

The general shock and widespread disgust at these events were best demonstrated by Beethoven, who had just finished his third symphony and had dedicated it to Napoleon for being the embodiment of egalitarian attitudes. On hearing that Napoleon was being crowned emperor, Beethoven angrily scratched out his name (the score has been preserved, ensuring that Beethoven's revulsion can be seen forever), and the piece became known as *Sinfonia Eroica* – in Italian, the Heroic Symphony.

37. NAPOLEON HAD A BIG WEAKNESS

Napoleon's greatest weakness was not a flaw in his character but a woman called Josephine de Beauharnais. Perhaps the best-known quote in this context is the one that came in his curt reply when she wanted some amorous attention, and Napoleon was said to be busy planning a battle: 'Not tonight, Josephine.'

It is highly unlikely that the story is true because, in reality, Napoleon was besotted with her. Josephine was six years older than Napoleon and already an accomplished power player when they met. In the 1790s, he was an unsophisticated young man with little experience of women.

Marie-Josèphe-Rose Tascher, known as Josephine, was born in 1763 on the French island of Martinique to a family of plantation owners. The family had fallen on hard times, and she married the wealthy Viscount Alexandre de Beauharnais to resolve their money problems. They had two children, but the marriage was not a happy one. Viscount Alexandre was imprisoned and executed during The Terror; Josephine was also imprisoned and scheduled for execution but was later released.

Josephine went on to become one of the most prominent women in France. Glamorous and well connected, she was rumoured to be the mistress of powerful men. For whatever reasons, she seems to have thought that Napoleon, then a rising star, was a useful person to attract, and she was a whole lot more pragmatic than Napoleon, who acted like a love-sick teenager. When Napoleon's family found out he was courting an older woman with children from another marriage, they were not best pleased.

It was clear that at the start of the relationship, she was the one wearing the trousers. When the newly married Napoleon went on campaign to conquer Italy, Josephine amused herself by having an affair and had to be forced to join her husband.

The tipping point seems to have been his return from Egypt, when an older, more mature Napoleon began to lead the relationship. There had been screaming matches and threats of divorce, and yet there she was by Napoleon's side at his imperial coronation.

However, a few years later, Josephine was menopausal, and while Napoleon still loved her, he needed a male heir to carry on his newly created imperial dynasty. So that he could marry into one of Europe's royal families, they divorced in 1810. Considering that he had 'married a womb', he didn't bother to turn up for his marriage to Marie-Louise of Austria. While she did deliver Napoleon's much desired son, his heart was still with Josephine, who despite being his ex-wife, continued to have her own palace and the title of empress.

In 1814, Josephine was still a natural at making great connections and was seen walking with Tsar Alexander of Russia in her garden. However, that promenade was to cost her dearly as she caught pneumonia and died. When Napoleon heard the news, he locked himself in his room for two days. Years later, on his death bed, she was in his final thoughts.

38. The White Cliffs of Dover Taunted Napoleon

By 1803, the one major power Napoleon had yet to conquer was Britain. His flair for manoeuvre on the battlefield was countered by the fact that to get to Britain, he needed ships. An amphibious invasion of a country is horrendously expensive, but Napoleon had just received 60 million francs from the Louisiana Purchase (huge areas of French territory in North America were sold to the United States, which more than doubled its size).

With this injection of cash, a massive effort was made to prepare for the invasion of Britain. Literally hundreds of barges were built, destined to be the troop transports to carry 200,000 French soldiers across the Channel. Because Napoleon knew this was the optimal time to conquer this most insistent of enemies, no expense was spared.

Napoleon wasn't frightened by new technologies. Anything that might help to ensure the success of the invasion was worthy of consideration. It was suggested that a tunnel to Britain could be dug – or that the troops might be sent over in hot air balloons. Both ideas were shelved as being completely impractical, but they showed the level of ambition and the technical difficulties that had prevented the successful invasion of England over the previous seven centuries.

A plan of this scale couldn't be hidden from the British; their first and most effective reaction was to use the Royal Naval to blockade French ports. But the British government couldn't assume that this alone would work and also ordered the construction of fortifications along England's south coast. The

Royal Military Canal, 28 miles long, was built in southern England as part of the plan to stop Napoleon, and better communications were ensured with the construction of semaphore stations to the south coast.

It was August of 1804 when Napoleon inspected his troops at Boulogne. They were well trained and well equipped – and a much larger force than anything Britain could muster. If they made it across the Channel, it was hard to see anything other than a French victory. However, the troop transports were slow and cumbersome and would be sitting ducks for the Royal Navy, so naval dominance of the Channel (or a Channel guaranteed to be empty of British warships) was required. This turned out to be the Achilles' heel of the plan. Napoleon was the foremost general of his day, but he never could get the better of the Royal Navy. In the period 1803–05, the French Navy's only goal was to beat the Royal Navy, a goal in which it singularly failed. As a result, it can be said that the Royal Navy (led by Nelson) saved Britain from invasion.

In the 1850s, a statue was erected in Boulogne to honour Napoleon's army. It became the point of arrival for many of the British troops heading for the trenches of the First World War. Tens of thousands of those men were met by a statute commemorating a potential attack on their country by the country they were then protecting.

39. Napoleon Had an Austrian Nemesis

Because these wars covered most of the European continent, each country tends to look at events from its own point of view. Therefore, the name Karl Ludwig Johann Josef Lorenz of Austria doesn't mean much in Britain.

Karl Ludwig, etc., conveniently known as Archduke Charles, was a brilliant Austrian general who fought more campaigns against the French in Europe than anyone else. He was the third son of the Holy Roman Emperor Leopold II and, as such, was unlikely to become emperor himself. The two most probable careers for spare heirs were in the church or in the army; Charles chose the latter. In the Wars of the First Coalition, he not only checked French advances in the Netherlands but also rolled them back (Fact 13). This was particularly impressive because it was his first major campaign. He was only in his early twenties (he was a few years younger than Napoleon), and he achieved all of this while suffering from epilepsy.

In the year 1796, the French were outmanoeuvred in the Rhineland, and two French armies were heavily defeated. These defeats took place at the hands of Archduke Charles. The same thing happened a year later: Napoleon was distracted elsewhere, and some of his northern Italian conquests were retaken by the archduke, who in the same campaigning season also marched on Switzerland and pushed new French forces out of the Rhineland – again.

By the time of the Wars of the Third Coalition, Archduke Charles was simply the go-to general for an Austrian victory. When Napoleon scored victories over Austria in 1805, it was because Charles was in

Italy protecting those lands from a potential French attack.

The two opposing military giants of this era were Napoleon and Wellington, but in a way, Archduke Charles combined the best of both of them. Like Napoleon, he excelled in speedy troop deployments and was a master of outmanoeuvring the enemy. But the archduke was also an administrator and planner, one who worried about logistics, which was one of Wellington's key abilities. His talent for logistics can be seen when, following the Austrian defeats during the Third Coalition, he became involved in the restructuring of the army, recognising it as old-fashioned and in need of improvement.

These reforms hadn't properly come into play in 1809 when he faced Napoleon. This campaign had victories on both sides, showing that Napoleon was by no means unbeatable; however, by the end of the campaign, Napoleon had come out on top. After another Austrian defeat, Charles hung up his spurs. By this time, he had been campaigning regularly for more than fifteen years.

Archduke Charles watched other generals go on to finally defeat Napoleon, but by then he was leading a quiet life. In 1815, he married Princess Henrietta and they had seven children. He became the Duke of Teschen in 1822 and died in 1847, aged seventy-five.

40. THE OLD GUARD WAS THE BEST GUARD

By 1804–05, Napoleon had been leading troops for a decade. Some of the men in his ranks had been with him from the first campaigns and had followed him to Italy, Egypt and beyond. Napoleon's elite body guard was known, at first, as the Consular Guard but, later, as the Imperial Guard. This in turn was split by experience into the Young, Middle and Old Guard; it was the Old Guard who were Napoleon's most feared troops.

In the beginning, Napoleon's personal guard would have been in the hundreds, then the low thousands but, as the number of his achievements grew, so did this elite group. By 1812, it numbered 100,000 and was an army in its own right.

Membership of the Old Guard was a prized military honour. A privilege reserved for them alone was the right to complain about any facet of the military without fear of reprimand. Some even complained when Napoleon was present. Within their own forces, they were *Les Grognards*, the grumblers.

Yet, for all their grumbling, they never wavered and always did as ordered on the field of battle. They faced annihilation at the Battle of Waterloo when, for the only time in its history, the Middle Guard broke and retreated without orders. However, the Old and Young Guard stood firm, allowing the rest of Napoleon's forces (and Napoleon himself) to leave the battlefield. They survived but had been nearly wiped out by cannon fire and cavalry charges.

41. THE GREAT BEAR WOKE UP – AND DITHERED

Although Russia had been part of the earlier wars, it was the Wars of the Third Coalition that were to make a huge impact on this great nation. Just a century earlier, the tsars had been looked down on as semi-barbaric, scraping a living on the edges of Europe. However, thanks to the impressive achievements of Peter and then Catherine the Great, the nation at last had become seen, somewhat begrudgingly, as an equal to the other major European powers.

For most of the wars with France, the country was led by Tsar Alexander I, one of Russia's most mediocre rulers. He won some battles but lost plenty too (and some of those defeats were major). He could be political, but he was no great statesman. Indeed, from 1804 to 1812, he changed Russia's status in relation to Napoleon multiple times – at one point acting as neutral peace maker, later as France's ally and, eventually, as Napoleon's enemy. He said he wanted to do something about serfdom, but nothing was done, and the serfs remained indentured servants for most of the rest of the nineteenth century.

As an absolute monarch, Alexander was surrounded by fawning courtiers and was regularly told that he was the new Alexander the Great. He was no such thing, but, on paper at least, he had an impressive list of titles. Not only was he Tsar of Russia, he was also the Grand Duke of Finland and the first Russian King of Poland (well, the bits that weren't now part of Prussia). However, this was against the backdrop of his diplomatic dithering and some serious defeats (which will be mentioned in later facts).

His changes of heart and strange decisions brought the Austrian foreign minister, Metternich, to the conclusion that Alexander was mad. The British and French found him exasperating and tiresome; it seems only Thomas Jefferson (the American statesman) wholly approved of him. Some of his behaviours may have been his attempt to compensate for the fact that his father, Tsar Paul I, had been a weak ruler, unloved even by his own mother (Catherine the Great).

Alexander came to power at the age of just twenty-three and reigned during a politically tumultuous period in Europe, a period that taxed all the powers and reshaped the borders of nations. Unlike Britain, Alexander did not have the luxury of a government to assist him; he was an autocratic tsar, and all decisions flowed through him. Even Alexander the Great would have had difficulty dealing with the constantly fluctuating state of affairs that prevailed at this time. Alexander I, however, paraded around in a general's uniform, pretending to be something he was not.

Alexander would rule until 1825, having survived a number of revolts and two failed kidnapping attempts (which led him to become ever more suspicious and less inclined to introduce the liberal reforms so desperately needed in Russian society). On a trip to southern Russia, he caught typhus and died at the age of forty-seven.

42. The French Navy Led a Great Game of Cat and Mouse

In 1805, Napoleon came up with a novel idea to weaken British coastal defences and allow his much sought after invasion of Britain. The first step in his bold plan of action required two fleets to break out from their British blockades in French ports and dash across the Atlantic. The fleets would rendezvous in the West Indies (British territory), invade a couple of islands and then, before the Royal Navy arrived, speed back across the Atlantic, finish off what few remaining vessels the British had in the Channel – and then launch his invasion.

It was possibly the most breathtaking plan in naval history. Crossing the Atlantic was never guaranteed to be an easy trip; to do it twice, with the world's most powerful navy giving chase, was a huge gamble.

The two French admirals in charge of the fleets were Villeneuve and Ganteaume. Villeneuve managed to slip past the British blockade by setting sail in the middle of the night, doing so with no lights – an impressive feat in itself. Ganteaume wasn't able to fool the Royal Navy and asked permission from Napoleon to battle his way out of port. Napoleon refused and Ganteaume's ships remained where they were.

Unaware of this, Villeneuve set sail under the assumption that the two fleets would meet at Martinique as planned. Meanwhile, Nelson had no idea where the rogue French fleet was or where it might be heading, a situation that spread panic in Britain (even the stock market went down). Nelson was not helped by false sightings and rumour. However, once he realised that the French objective was the Caribbean, Nelson travelled from Gibraltar to Barbados in just three weeks. Shortly after his arrival, he realised the two fleets had come within a hundred miles of each other, but the French had slipped away again.

The good news for Nelson was that the French hadn't launched an invasion of the West Indies, so those territories were safe. But by now the British realised that Villeneuve was arching back across the Atlantic, and the defences of the Channel coast had to be bolstered. A fleet was sent to intercept Villeneuve, but once again he slipped past the British, this time aided by fog. When the two fleets finally did meet, neither one attacked the other. Villeneuve was able to keep his fleet intact and return to a safe port, having carried out one of the most impressive naval manoeuvres in history. While he had suffered no defeat, he had failed in both stages of the plan. The West Indies remained British, and a British fleet remained in the Channel.

Napoleon's own over optimistic planning was, of course, not the problem. No, he blamed everything on his navy, remarking, 'How small England will become when France gets two or three admirals who are willing to face death!'

43. Napoleon Wondered What to Do with a Spare Army

When no invasion of Britain seemed possible, Napoleon was left wondering what to do with his huge, well-equipped force in Boulogne. In late August of 1805, Napoleon took it to Austria. The Austrians, assuming there would be a French attack in Italy, had positioned their best forces further south, but they were in alliance with Russia, which had promised to send troops to bolster Austria's defences. The Russians, however, wavered and no force of any useful size arrived before the end of the campaign.

Napoleon smashed into Austria and skirmished with its army in a series of small engagements, which resulted in the Austrians having ever less room for manoeuvre. These allowed Napoleon (with Ney and Murat) to retain the initiative. It all culminated in the Battle of Ulm where the French outnumbered the Austrians two to one.

Ulm was where Karl Mack von Leiberich had concentrated his 40,000 troops. Some of his heavy cavalry managed to break out, but after three days of fighting and the French tightening their grip, he was forced to surrender. 4,000 of his men died and 25,000 were captured.

Mack had been a prisoner of war in France in 1797, so it must have been a bitter blow to fall to the French again. After the (future) Battle of Austerlitz, Mack seemed to lose the will to fight; he was convicted of cowardice, stripped of his rank and spent two years in an Austrian prison, before being reinstated in the army as lieutenant marshal.

44. An Admiral Died and a Legend Was Born

On 21 October 1805, a Franco-Spanish fleet, led by Admiral Villeneuve, met Admiral Lord Nelson's fleet off Cape Trafalgar in the south-west of Spain.

By this time, Nelson had a well-deserved reputation for the use of innovative tactics, on this occasion attacking the enemy fleet from a perpendicular angle, rather than side-by-side as was traditional. He also trusted his officers to follow out the spirit of his orders and improvise if need be. Villeneuve, by comparison, had his fleet lined up in the standard way and couldn't come up with a counter plan to Nelson's attack.

The Royal Navy was slightly outnumbered, and some of the French and Spanish flagships were considerably larger than Nelson's *Victory*, something that had never worried Nelson in the past. Despite all his previous victories and successes, this was the first time that Nelson was the leading admiral, but he neither expected nor required input from less able senior officers. Nelson was in charge.

As the Royal Navy engaged, Nelson raised a signal that said, 'ENGLAND EXPECTS THAT EVERY MAN WILL DO HIS DUTY'. It should be pointed out that at the time (and contrary to current sensitivities), the terms 'England' and 'Britain' were interchangeable, so no offence was intended or taken.

By midday the battle was in full swing. HMS *Victory* 'locked masts' with the French ship *Redoubtable*, and it was here, in the furious fighting, that a French marksman shot Nelson, fatally wounding him. The muskets of the time were not that accurate, particularly on a moving ship, so it is likely that the shooter was simply aiming at the group of officers on deck. It was probably blind luck that his musket ball found this target.

It's a myth that Nelson had a death wish and was walking around with all his medals. His jacket had cloth versions of his medals, and far from standing around waiting to be shot, he was on deck issuing orders. Nelson was frequently wounded in battle, not because of a death wish but because of his energetic style of leadership, which won battles but, ultimately, lost him his life.

While the victory was overwhelming, it was the storm that rose up almost immediately afterwards that caused even more damage to the Franco-Spanish fleet. Some ships were forced to be sunk after they suffered the double damage inflicted by battle and storm. Of the 15,000 casualties suffered that day, more than 3,000 were drowned in the storm. The Franco-Spanish fleet lost twenty-two ships out of forty-one, whereas the Royal Navy didn't lose a single one. However, the death of their foremost naval officer was a bitter blow.

The battle was one of the most decisive naval victories during the Wars of the Third Coalition and firmly established Britain's supremacy at sea. Nelson's victory at Trafalgar had been so emphatic that no enemy fleet presented any serious challenge to the Royal Navy until the Battle of Jutland, 111 years later.

45. Nelson Took Wolsey's Place

After the Battle of Trafalgar, many of the British dead were taken to Gibraltar where they were buried. Nelson, however, had been put in a barrel of brandy to preserve him. At Gibraltar his body was moved to a lead-lined coffin filled with aqua vitae (ethanol).

The body was eventually placed inside a wooden coffin made from the main mast of *L'Orient*, the French flagship that had exploded during the Battle of the Nile. Nelson had been so gravely wounded that he was not expected to survive, and the coffin prepared for him then was still considered to be appropriate a few years later.

Nelson's body lay in state at Greenwich for three days, and thousands came to pay their respects. On 9 January 1806, crowds of mourners, including 30,000 soldiers, lined the route of the funeral procession, which started from the Admiralty and wound its way to St Paul's Cathedral. The funeral cortège consisted of thirty-two admirals and 10,000 soldiers and was so long that when the front of it had arrived at St Paul's, the rear hadn't even set off.

St Paul's was draped in the flags of captured French and Spanish ships. The service lasted for four hours and was attended by some 7,000 people, including dukes, earls, admirals and captains, along with seamen and marines from the HMS *Victory*. When Nelson was interred at St Paul's, he was placed inside an elaborate sarcophagus originally intended for Cardinal Wolsey.

46. AUSTERLITZ WAS NAPOLEON'S GREATEST VICTORY

The Battle of Austerlitz took place in what was then part of Austria and is now part of the Czech Republic. It is also known as the Battle of the Three Emperors (those of France, Russia and the Holy Roman Empire) and shows just how much was at stake. The Austrians, in particular, desperately needed to win as Napoleon had just captured Vienna.

Napoleon was outnumbered, with 30 per cent fewer troops than the enemy. However, he had scouted the land and deliberately evacuated the Pratzen Plateau, which he correctly guessed would be the natural mustering point for the Austro-Russian (allied) army. It was there he observed, 'If the Russian force leaves the Pratzen Heights in order to go to the right side, they will certainly be defeated.'

The battle started early on the morning of 2 December 1805, and, as predicted, the allies moved off the plateau to attack Napoleon's flank, which weakened their centre. Shortly after this, Napoleon ordered General Soult to attack this vulnerable mid-point, effectively breaking the allied army in two. The Russians countered with heavy cavalry charges, capturing a French golden eagle standard. Losing the regimental flag was shameful, but it was the only one to be lost by the French that day. They replied with their own heavy cavalry and barrage after barrage of canister shot. These packs of iron balls shredded the lines of Russian infantry, and they broke in flight. The French chased the retreating troops and inflicted further casualties.

As this was happening to the south of the battlefield, to the north the Austrians were similarly fighting

THE NAPOLEONIC WARS IN 100 FACTS

furiously. Six French cavalry regiments were sent into battle, and five of them were pushed back. However, once the Austrian lines were broken, there was a chaotic rout. As the French artillery continued to pound the retreating men, the barrage broke up the ice on the surrounding rivers and lakes. As a result, many men drowned in the freezing waters. 15,000 allied soldiers were killed or wounded and a further 12,000 were captured.

Austerlitz is one of those classic battlefield engagements that are reviewed again and again. Napoleon planned everything, and the battle had unfolded like clockwork. It was arguably Napoleon's greatest victory and demonstrated, yet again, his inestimable superiority over (admittedly) average foes. The Third Coalition was effectively destroyed by this battle. Both Russia and Austria were forced to sign a humiliating truce, and the Holy Roman Emperor, Francis II, abdicated shortly afterwards, bringing to a close this ancient, 1,000-year-old empire. As he watched his empire expire, Francis II bitterly remarked, 'The British are dealers of human flesh. They pay others to fight at their place.'

While this comment overlooked British naval victories, it was true that in terms of mainland Europe, Britain had so far contributed little apart from paying for coalition military expenses.

Cannon captured at Austerlitz were melted down and turned into the column now at the Place Vendôme in Paris. It was Napoleon's answer to Trajan's column in Rome.

47. NAPOLEON UNDERSTOOD THE PROPAGANDA WAR

The Napoleonic Wars were not the first wars to use the medium of print for propaganda purposes. *The Times*, for example (started in 1785 as *The Daily Universal Register*), was not above bias. But this particular era of conflict excelled at printing scurrilous opinions and defamatory cartoons. The leaders of the age knew the power of the press. As Napoleon once said, 'Four hostile newspapers are more to be feared than a thousand bayonets.'

However, it's not just opinion pieces that influence; imagery is often more powerful and, undoubtedly, lingers longer. Napoleon understood this and was no stranger to self-aggrandisement. In Fact 26, mention was made of the famous painting of a heroic *Napoleon Crossing the Alps*, a portrayal that bore no relation to the truth of that challenging journey to what would be his great victory at Marengo. But the truth would not inspire respect and admiration.

Napoleon made sure his coronation as emperor was immortalised in oil paintings, and both he and Josephine had regal portraits of themselves in their splendid imperial robes. While Napoleon didn't plan his own tomb, it continued the themes of power and supremacy, this time with Napoleon as an Adonis, a god among men. Brilliant general he assuredly was, but physically he was a little on the pudgy side and had a crooked nose.

Napoleon had the twin advantages of being both a general and an absolute ruler; he was able to dictate and control the press. Britain did not provide its monarchs and leaders with the same benefits; it had a freer press, and parliamentary democracy meant magazines like *Punch* could draw witheringly satirical cartoons of friend and foe alike.

Napoleon's nickname 'Boney' was a British invention designed to conjure up antipathy. John Bull was the visual summary of what was then considered to be the stereotypical Englishman: he was a patriot, plump, down-to-earth and a lover of beer (not a lot's changed in 225 years). At the time it was thought that having some meat on your bones was a good thing; therefore, horrible old 'Boney' was either a wraith to be feared or a midget to be mocked.

To set the record straight, Napoleon wasn't short. The misunderstanding arose because French measurements were different to British ones, and we now know that Napoleon was a little taller than the average man of his time. However, well-fed British aristocrats tended to be much taller than the average peasant, so Napoleon would have looked diminutive standing next to someone like the Duke of Wellington. But that didn't stop grotesque imagery of a jumped-up dwarf with a hooked nose being used as the standard depiction of Napoleon in the British (and other countries') press. He is often portrayed as compensating for his lack of stature with comically large hats and boots. The idea that Napoleon was short still exists to this day, all thanks to scandalous British propaganda from 200 years ago.

48. THE BRITISH FOUGHT THE FRENCH ON LAND ... FINALLY

After Napoleon's stunning success at Austerlitz, it seemed he could achieve anything, so in 1806, he ordered his army to invade the last major territory in Italy not under his control: the Kingdom of Naples.

If Russia and the Holy Roman Empire couldn't thwart the French, Naples, a small kingdom, stood no chance. King Francis II had counted on British support, but they didn't have enough troops to stop the French and decided to withdraw by ship, leaving the Italians to their fate. This was a pragmatic decision by the British but a pretty ignominious one.

However, what happened in southern Italy was a microcosm of Napoleon's ongoing dilemma. Winning a battle and bringing a defeated enemy to the negotiating table was one thing, but ensuring the capitulation of the population as a whole was a different matter entirely. Just like Egypt nearly a decade earlier, and just like Spain a few years later, the French could win battles but not dominate the population.

As the French were unable to sustain their authority, the British returned with a small force of just over 5,000 men, led by Lieutenant General John Stuart. After successfully landing his troops, he went in search of the remaining French troops in the area. The French commander, Reynier, came out to meet this British expeditionary force, determined to drive it into the sea.

They met at Maida (in Calabria), but Stuart had been the first to arrive and held a low ridge, having anchored his troops on higher ground. As the French advanced, Stuart ordered his men to hold fire. He waited until the last second before unleashing close range (and therefore more accurate) volley fire. The instant decimation of the French ranks led to panic, and the battle was over relatively quickly. At the end, about half of the French troops were either dead, wounded or captured. It was a minor victory, but after all of Britain's naval victories, it was a much-needed success on land.

The French scored a victory by winning the siege of the Italian town of Gaeta, but that was their last success of the campaign. While ensuring that there was no invasion of Sicily, Stuart also cultivated the general disenchantment of the locals into a full-scale rebellion against the French. The Battle of Maida was, by the standards of the era, a small engagement, but it was important as it highlighted the limitations of Napoleon's ability to enforce his rule on the population as a whole. It also proved that the British weren't just good sailors.

To honour his victory, John Stuart was made Count of Maida, and he was lavished with titles and honours. He would later return to the south of Italy and again block all French attempts (led by Murat, the new king of Naples) from any further expansion in the area.

49. THE BEST WAY TO WIN WAS TO INVADE ARGENTINA

By 1806, Britain had been at war almost constantly for well over a decade. Her continental allies were continually being humbled by French armies, and her own contributions to the war, thus far, had been mainly naval victories. However, William Pitt and Sir Home Riggs Popham had been kicking around ideas to weaken France's main ally, Spain.

Spain's South American empire was largely undefended. Trying to resist a British invasion there would take Spanish troops away from the resources that Napoleon could use in Europe. So, in short, it was decided that the best way to win a war against France in Europe was to invade Argentina in South America.

These operations were referred to as the British invasions of the Río de la Plata. Britain achieved early success when it captured Buenos Aires, one of the key cities in the area, and held it for over a month. When the invaders were ejected, it wasn't thanks to the arrival of Spanish troops but to an uprising of the local population.

In 1807, the British responded by sending a larger invasion force, this time successfully storming Montevideo, where they stayed for a few months just to prove a point. Shortly afterwards, the British sent a third force back to Buenos Aires, but after heavy fighting with a combined force of Spanish soldiers standing side-by-side with the local militia, they were pushed back and suffered more than 50 per cent casualties.

The British lost this campaign. It was an ambitious plan that had assumed resistance could only be achieved by Spanish regular troops. In fact, it was the bravery of the locals that saved Río de la Plata from becoming part of the British Empire.

The repercussions of this attempted invasion were unforeseen by everyone. The Spanish were, at first, overjoyed that their colonies had resisted so resolutely. However, those same colonies felt that their actions had earned them the right to be considered the equal of their colonial masters in Spain.

The Spanish were, at this time, also having serious trouble with a French invasion of their own country so could do little (more on that later). By 1810, the South American colonies felt confident enough to carry out their own revolution (the May Revolution), which removed the Spanish Viceroy and set up a local government for the first time. This led, in July 1816, to the declaration of independence for the United Provinces of South America, which later became known as Argentina. At the time, some of the ex-Spanish colonies were at war with each other but, overall, shrugging off the old colonial overlord was seen as beneficial.

The irony then was that while Britain lost the campaign, it achieved its goals of weakening Spain and distracting Spanish priorities and forces. Another irony is that today in Argentina, Britain's actions of 1806–07 are seen as the trigger for independence and are widely considered to have been a good thing.

50. THE FOURTH COALITION INTENDED TO STOP NAPOLEON

There was no period of peace between the Third and Fourth Coalitions, and after Austerlitz, Napoleon dominated most of Western Europe. One of his oldest enemies, Austria, now witnessed its capital, Vienna, being used as a base for French operations. While not everything had gone Napoleon's way (notably Trafalgar, a failed invasion attempt of Britain and the continued insurrection in southern Italy), he had become the most powerful man in Europe since the time of Charlemagne, a thousand years earlier.

To try and staunch the flow of French power across the continent, a new coalition was hastily created from the ashes of Austerlitz. Again, Britain was at the forefront of negotiations and funding. William Pitt had died in early 1806, and the new Prime Minister, Lord Grenville, was Prime Minister for about as long as the coalition he oversaw. Because Austria had been forced into a peace treaty with France, it could do nothing more than sit on the sidelines and lick its wounds.

Despite Frederick William III's careful attempts to avoid confrontation, Prussia knew it was the next target. Faced with certain war, it was decided that it would be prudent to join the Fourth Coalition (1806–07). Fearing the worst for their own countries, Saxony, Sweden and Russia joined as well. France, meanwhile, could count on the Federation of the Rhine, the old enemy states of Prussia and, of course, Spain, as well as other territories dominated by France.

Would Prussia's involvement be enough to stop Napoleon this time?

51. The Battle of Jena Was Really Two Battles

With a Fourth Coalition in existence and Prussia now openly hostile to France, Napoleon wasted no time and invaded with an army of 70,000. His goal was a decisive victory over the Prussians, who had too often been on the fringes of anti-French coalitions.

The campaign culminated on 14 October 1806, with not one but two battles – miles apart – on the same day. The French list of commanders is a 'who's who' of the most dynamic generals of the day: Napoleon, Murat, Ney, Davout – the list goes on and on. These commanders led an army that had been honed in battle during long years of combat. The Prussians, on paper at least, had nearly twice as many men, but the army hadn't evolved its tactics since the era of Frederick the Great (about fifty years earlier), and they were led by the seventy-one-year-old Duke of Brunswick.

The Prussians had around 60,000 men in both battles. While Napoleon had 40,000 at Jena, at Auerstedt the French had fewer than 30,000 and so were outnumbered two-to-one.

Marshal Ney had a rash side, and it showed at Jena where he started the engagement by attacking the Prussians without orders to do so. His initial attack was successful, but the full weight of the Prussian army and its artillery bore down on him. Thanks to Ney's impatience, Napoleon had to abandon his original plan and ordered his forces to support Ney. Even as his original strategy unravelled, Napoleon remained cool and decisive.

Napoleon then carried out a classic pincer movement, which broke the flanks of the Prussian army. As the

French threatened to surround them, the Prussians had no option but to flee. 15,000 Prussians were captured, and they suffered some 10,000 casualties versus 7,500 for the French.

Meanwhile, the French generals Davout and Gudin were fighting around the town of Hassenhausen, near Auerstedt. The Prussians had gathered a sizeable force, which was led by Schmettau and Brunswick and supported by General Blücher's cavalry.

The French formed anti-cavalry squares, but Blücher attacked anyway and was, predictably, repulsed. The Prussian infantry advanced but were simply out-performed by the French veteran troops. The Prussians could have out-gunned the French, but it never came to that as the attack failed to use the Prussian's full numerical advantage, in addition to which, both Brunswick and Schmettau were seriously wounded in the battle.

Communications in the Prussian army broke down, and its retreat turned into a rout. By the time Frederick William III had ordered a retreat, it was already happening, and while the Battle of Auerstedt finished first, by the end of the day, Prussia had been defeated twice. Its army was in tatters.

Napoleon was so surprised at Davout's even greater victory than his own that he first thought Davout might be exaggerating, but on realising the true extent of the victory, he lavished him with praise. Napoleon had yet another new territory to add to his ever-expanding list of conquests.

52. Napoleon Was a Great General but a Terrible Economist

After Napoleon's victories in Prussia, he clashed with Russia and then spent some time in his new northern German territories. It was in Berlin in late 1806 that he issued the Berlin Decree, which forbade the import of goods from the British Empire into any of his territories.

By this time Napoleon's lands covered a huge swathe of Europe. From the south of Spain to the Baltic Sea, all French allies and subjugated nations now had to turn their back on British trade. As far as Britain was concerned, Europe was closed for business. Napoleon did this in retaliation for Britain's continued blockade of French (and their allies') ports. The shooting war had ended for now, but the trade war was just getting started.

At first glance, Napoleon's so-called Continental System made sense. Continental Europe had been trading internally for centuries and had enjoyed economic growth. This, along with the resources of French colonies, combined with the economies of Italy and Austria, should have been more than enough to keep Napoleon's empire going.

Neutral shipping became a target for both antagonistic powers. This and the above embargo on British goods was reinforced a year later in the Milan Decree (Napoleon travelled a lot), which led to the United States feeling aggrieved by certain actions of the Royal Navy. The effects of these decisions were far reaching.

There were, however, some fundamental problems with Napoleon's plan. Although British trade was seriously affected, particularly in the first few years when some exports dropped by a massive 50 per cent, it shouldn't be forgotten that Britannia ruled the waves. With a growing global empire and trade agreements with many nations not under Napoleon's power, Britain found that it could absorb the blow of Napoleon's embargo.

However, the Continent couldn't say the same thing about the absence of British trade. Britain, at this time, was starting to industrialise; it was the first country in the world to do so. This meant it could produce more goods at a cheaper price. Europe attempted to fill the gap of cheap British imports by demanding more from its ancient and inefficient supply chains; they simply couldn't cope. Food prices started to go up in France, and those places where ship building or maritime trade were carried out slumped into economic depression.

As the decline in trade bit ever deeper, the system broke down. Britain could easily smuggle goods into countries resentful of the French embargo; some countries, like Portugal and Sweden, didn't join in the first place. The more local leaders turned a blind eye to British smuggling, the more it helped Britain and hurt Napoleon's economic plan. In short, if the idea of the trade embargo was to hurt the enemy, with no cost to the French, Napoleon's plan singularly failed.

The French economy, which had been tumultuous ever since the revolution, was further badly damaged by political mismanagement. Napoleon's Continental System was eventually scrapped in 1814, much to everyone's relief.

53. THERE WERE MANY SECRETS IN THE NAPOLEONIC ERA

By the time of the Napoleonic Wars, codes and secret communications had come a long way since the fifth century BC, when the Ancient Greeks would tattoo a message onto the head of a slave and wait for the hair to grow back. The concept of codes and information warfare had been evolving even in pre-electronic times.

By the mid-eighteenth century, the French had developed the *Grande Chiffre*. This was a code that didn't just replace a letter with another letter or symbol, but one that actually encoded syllables with multiple variants of numbers. Add to this that the repetition of phrases was deliberately avoided and that names were usually replaced with other terms to prevent spies from guessing at words that could help them unlock the messages, and you have a reasonably sophisticated cipher. In order to put code breakers off track, words were sometimes misspelt, and most cunningly of all, messages often started and finished with a random selection of numbers just to make decryption harder.

Sir George Scovell was engaged to break French codes, and in 1811 this remarkable linguistic expert cracked it in two days. It turned out that the codes being used at this time were less sophisticated than those with higher levels of encryption that had been used previously. However, when the French correctly guessed that their codes had been broken, they reintroduced a version of the *Grande Chiffre*, which Scovell never entirely cracked but understood well enough to get key pieces of information. On one occasion, he gave Wellington enough intelligence to anticipate French actions at the Battle of Vitoria.

Napoleon was not without his own spies, best embodied by Joseph Fouché, Duke of Otranto. Another example of a Frenchman who nearly joined the clergy, Fouché learned his skills of survival and espionage by climbing the greasy pole of power during the French Revolution. In 1794, he was powerful enough to openly disagree and challenge Robespierre, although he was nearly executed in 1795. It was under Napoleon, however, that he found his natural role when he became the Minister of Police and spent years hunting down groups that were plotting either to assassinate or overthrow Napoleon. There were plenty of them.

Indeed, Fouché's ability to uncover coups and cabals led Napoleon to distrust him. Could it be that he was inventing them to make himself look good? Or was Fouché behind some of these plots himself? For a time Fouché was pushed into the role of senator, but his network of spies meant he was better informed than the new Minister of Police, so Napoleon reinstated him and later made him Interior Minister and Duke of Otranto (along with a few other titles). Napoleon, on a number of occasions, demoted and sidelined Fouché, but the man was just too good at his job to shun for long.

Fouché and Scovell are symbolic of all the shadowy intrigue that went on throughout this era, much of which has been lost to history.

54. THE TREATY OF TILSIT WAS SIGNED ON A RAFT IN THE MIDDLE OF A RIVER

After the battles of Jena and Austerlitz, the French moved east. In this era of political history, Prussia had a common border with Russia, and so Napoleon, for the first time ever, entered Russian territory where the local Polish population treated him as a liberator. Napoleon already had Polish Legions in his forces, but new recruits swelled his ranks. He subsequently created a new Northern Legion, which was not exclusively Polish but was dominated by that ethnicity. Later on, he would create the Duchy of Warsaw, a small Polish state.

By late 1806, the Russians and the French had skirmished and fought minor engagements, but as neither side had properly committed themselves to battle, the results were inconclusive. The Baltic coast has cold and icy winters, so the weather further hindered the ability to keep a large army in the field.

Under the circumstances, the main clash between Napoleon and the Russians would have to wait until June of 1807, when the two forces met at Friedland. A few days earlier, some of Napoleon's generals had tried a direct attack on a Russian army at Heilsberg, but the French were bloodily repulsed, and Napoleon understood that the blunt battering-ram approach was unlikely to work on the Russians. Meanwhile, at Friedland, French General Lannes kept the Russians fixed and fully occupied, a ploy that risked attack by a larger force but which allowed time for the rest of the French forces to arrive to strike the killer blow. Once Lannes had managed to entice the Russians into crossing the river on pontoon bridges, it became much harder for them to disengage. At the height of the battle, more than 50,000 Russians had crossed over, which meant that they were now committed to stand and fight.

The French attacked from multiple directions and were supported by cannon fire. Restricted by the bends in the river, the Russians had run out of room to manoeuvre. Of the 85,000 Russian troops, nearly half were killed, injured or captured. It was another emphatic victory for Napoleon, and it forced Tsar Alexander I to the peace table.

The negotiation started off very well with Alexander saying, 'I hate the English as much as you do.' Napoleon replied, 'In that case, peace is as good as made.'

The peace agreement was signed at the city of Tilsit on the Neman River, where a raft had been anchored in the centre of the river so that neither emperor would have an advantage over the other. For once Napoleon chose not to humiliate a vanquished foe, and Russia was given concessions in return for joining the Continental System. The Prussians were not as lucky. In another peace treaty signed shortly afterwards, huge swathes of Prussian territory were given to Russia or turned into a new Polish duchy. Tilsit was yet another treaty negotiated from a position of strength. Napoleon was at his pinnacle, reshaping Europe to his will.

55. FRANCE BETRAYED AN ALLY

For nearly a decade, every time France had gone to war, Spain was by its side. Just like the French, the Spanish had also suffered bitter defeats at the hands of the Royal Navy. Spain was a loyal and valued ally. Therefore, virtually everyone was left scratching their heads when Napoleon invaded the Iberian Peninsula in 1807.

The Iberian Peninsula consisted, then as now, of two countries: Spain and Portugal. Portugal's resistance to the Continental System and its long-term alliance with Britain (dating back to the fourteenth century and before, when English crusaders of the twelfth century helped to recapture Lisbon from the Moors) automatically made it Napoleon's enemy. Spain was also hesitant on the issue of the Continental System, but while this was the alleged cause for war, invasion seemed extreme for a country that had so generously supported Napoleon with both money and men.

Earlier in his career, Napoleon had believed Spain to be a 'hard nut' to crack, so exactly why he had a change of heart is hard to say. Common conjecture held that after all his recent victories, Napoleon began to believe his own hype. Austria, Prussia and Russia all had formidable military reputations, and they had been humbled by him in just a few years. Certainly there wasn't a lot of logic in Napoleon's decision to send General Junot across the Pyrenees. The initial attack went well, and French forces swept into the Iberian Peninsula.

The main Spanish army was underpaid, underequipped and pretty much leaderless, so it put up no real resistance. The government wasn't in much better shape. The king had abdicated and his son was installed in his place, but a number of governments-in-exile had sprung up to deal with the invasion from France and insurrection in the colonies (mainly in South America and, particularly, in Argentina). As well, they were all busy vying for power against other fragments of the government. In short, it was chaos. Despite all of this, Napoleon controlled the Spanish capital of Madrid for years, even installing his eldest brother Joseph as the King of Spain.

Meanwhile, the Portuguese managed to get both their fleet and their royal family out of the country and on their way to their colony of Brazil before the French arrived.

Without a regular fighting force, the Spanish began a campaign of guerrilla (a Spanish word meaning 'small war') warfare. Today we would call this an insurgency, and it wasn't pretty. French patrols were ambushed, tortured and killed. In order to frighten and intimidate, the mutilated bodies of French soldiers were left in places where their comrades would find them. Like all insurgencies, it caused major problems for the invaders and sapped French resources, but it was not able to oust the larger military force from the area. For that Spain would need its own ally with a regular army – and that turned out to be Britain.

56. Nobody Expected the Spanish Inquisition ... to End

The story of the Inquisition is a long and complex one, but the first area to come under its scrutiny was in twelfth-century France (for more on this, see *Deus Vult: a Concise History of the Crusades*). The most notorious version of these religious inquiries into potential heretics or apostates started in Spain in the late fifteenth century and never really went away until the nineteenth century.

The French Revolution caused real concerns in Spain. King Charles VII worried about how his people might regard the wealth and power not only of the monarchy but also of the Church. With this in mind, he took steps to clip the wings of the Inquisition.

The French had already shown a willingness to challenge centuries-old institutions, and it was under Joseph Bonaparte that the Inquisition was abolished once and for all ... sort of. When the Spanish regained control of their country, the new government dealt the death blow to this anachronistic regime.

However, the Inquisition still had a part to play in the 1820s and '30s, when it returned for just enough time to execute a teacher for suggesting so-called heretical ideas. That's right; the last person to be killed by the Spanish Inquisition was a teacher in 1834 ... after which it was finally abolished. The Inquisition exists today as 'The Congregation for the Doctrine of the Faith', a body that advises the Pope on issues of creed and doctrine. It hasn't killed anyone for nearly 200 years.

57. The New Coalition Hoped It Was Fifth Time Lucky

France's invasion of Spain triggered the creation of yet another coalition. For the first time since the First Coalition a decade earlier, Spain joined an allied coalition, signalling the biggest change to the alignment of sides in the new Fifth Coalition (1809). This consisted of Austria, Portugal, Spain and the United Kingdom.

Still reeling from the punitive measures in the Treaty of Schönbrunn, the Austrians had been forced to sit out the Wars of the Fourth Coalition, but they were by no means done fighting French domination. It wouldn't be an exaggeration to say that Napoleon was both feared and loathed, in equal measures, in the court in Vienna. However, Prussia, which had stood up to Napoleon in the Fourth Coalition, had been neutered and had lost nearly half of its territories as a result. So, during the Fifth Coalition, Prussia had to sit on the sidelines just as Austria had done during the Fourth.

Although initially successful, Napoleon's invasion plans were running into difficulty. Despite ploughing more and more troops into Spain, he was unable to bring the Iberian Peninsula to heel. The country was proving to be a bottomless pit in terms of men and resources. Because he needed to concentrate his efforts on this campaign, Napoleon had done his best to secure as many peaceful fronts as he could elsewhere. The Treaty of Tilsit had forged an unlikely but welcome alliance with Russia, one which was further reinforced in 1808 at the Congress of Erfurt. In this congress, France recognised Russia's recent conquest of Finland (a major blow to Sweden), which kept another potential ally out of the war.

Austria had a massive army, but its continued mobilisation cost a fortune, and Austria looked to Britain, yet again, to provide war loans. Westminster was only too happy to oblige. Because Britain was usually eager to support others in their fight against Napoleon, it was regarded as France's most persistent enemy throughout this period. Many of the victories won by other countries were actually funded by British loans and bonds.

Britain could afford to do this for several reasons. Firstly, Napoleon had failed to invade Britain, and therefore the nation was not forced to pay punitive tributes. Secondly, Britain's banking system was the most modern in the world and could effortlessly adjust interest rates via the Bank of England (although throughout this long war, they never changed from 5 per cent). Further, the empire ensured profits from trade and a strong trade surplus. Finally, industrialisation meant continued efficiencies in manufacturing, which led to further profits, which meant investors had the funds to support government loans to countries like Austria.

Spain was a novel theatre of war for all of the armies involved, but it was not the only one in the Wars of the Fifth Coalition. Battles took place across central Europe, and for the Austrians, it was a depressingly familiar situation as they once more faced French armies near their borders.

58. JOHN MOORE REPLACED WELLINGTON

For the first time since the First Coalition, an entire British army landed on the Continent in August of 1808. It was led by Arthur Wellesley and almost immediately went into action at the Battle of Roliça (in Portugal) in the Peninsular War (a war for the Iberian Peninsula within the Napoleonic Wars). The British army, supported by Portuguese soldiers, defeated a much smaller French army that was forced to beat a well-ordered but hasty retreat.

It was an encouraging start for Britain's new strategy. The French recognised that they had over extended their lines and, by the end of the month, had signed the Convention of Sintra, which allowed them to evacuate Portugal without a fight, all of their troops and equipment intact.

This seemed to be an easy and relatively bloodless win for Britain and Portugal ... and a pragmatic solution to France's occupation of Portugal. Nevertheless, this is not how it was seen in London, where there were concerns that a French defeat had been turned into an orderly retreat with full honours. The entire military leadership of the British forces in Portugal was told to return to Britain to explain its actions.

With Wellesley and the others on their way to London, Lieutenant General John Moore was put in charge of British forces on the Iberian Peninsula. Moore was a tough Scot, battle-hardened in combat from the time of the American Revolution; he was the perfect choice to pick up Wellesley's reigns. It was just unfortunate that as Wellington and his colleagues were leaving, Napoleon arrived in Spain with 200,000 troops. The French quickly crushed whatever remnants of Spanish army there were that dared to face them.

Moore knew he had to retreat, so he carefully led French Marshal Soult on a northerly route to the Spanish coast, where he used the winter weather and the difficult mountain terrain to his advantage. While Moore knew his men were suffering in the harsh conditions, he also knew it would be no less grim for the French trying to pursue them. When discipline broke down and British troops raided and looted Spanish towns, Moore got everyone back on track and kept his men plodding on through the freezing rain and dreadful conditions. He was determined to keep the army intact. When they finally reached the port of Corunna, the British could at last re-equip, now protected by Royal Navy cannon.

Soult finally caught up with Moore at Corunna. The two roughly equal sides fought just outside the small town of Elvina, which changed hands several times during the battle. Unfortunately, the British suffered heavy casualties from the French cannon set on nearby high ground, and it was one of these that killed Moore when he was struck by a cannon ball.

Ultimately, the French were pushed back, and thanks entirely to Moore's cool head and brilliant tactics over the long weeks of retreat, the British army remained a fighting force even as it embarked on Royal Navy ships.

59. DISASTER FOR BOTH SIDES RESULTED IN VICTORY FOR ONE

Austerlitz had been an emphatic victory for Napoleon, so it was a sign of both Austrian resilience and enmity to Napoleon that the country was back in the Fifth Coalition. Wagram, in Austria, lies to the north-east of Vienna. The Battle of Wagram was the largest fought so far in this era of almost continuous European warfare. It was also one of the most important engagements of the Napoleonic Wars, with both sides fielding over 150,000 troops.

No sooner had Napoleon won some glory in Spain than he quickly left the country, sensing he had won the battle but not the war. He left victory in the Peninsular War to others as he set his sights, yet again, on Austria.

This time the battlefield was a relatively flat plain and, unlike many other battlefields, had little in the way of key features. Napoleon got his troops across the Danube and attacked first on the evening of 4 July 1809. After some initial success, darkness fell, and the Austrians still held their ground. The real battle would commence the following day.

Archduke Charles (Fact 39) was again leading the Austrians, and he sensed that the initial skirmishes on the previous evening hadn't gone the way Napoleon had hoped, so he attacked with full force on the morning of 5 July. As the Austrians poured tens of thousands of men at Napoleon, his left flank buckled under the sheer weight of numbers and the ferocity of attack, triggering Napoleon's decision to send in his cavalry to stop the Austrian advance. It worked, and his right flank fared much better, resisting everything

Archduke Charles could throw at it. The rest of the day was attack and counterattack as the two armies bludgeoned each other into submission. The artillery units on both sides had wide fields of vision and were particularly lethal in this battle.

As the light faded on a bloody day, neither side had won. In fact, some French forces had retreated, and darkness gave them time to rally and return to the front lines. As 6 July dawned, the Austrians were already attacking; however, as the French were also about to set off for a dawn assault, the Austrians ran into battle-ready troops. There was no element of surprise, just intense volley fire from both sides.

Again, for most of the day, infantry advance was checked with cavalry, and artillery was used to support an assault or push back an attack. It was the Austrians who tired first. Some of their units had been fighting constantly for nine or ten hours; they had nothing left to give. Rather than risk annihilation, Charles knew it was better to keep his army intact. He had tried everything, but the French, battered and bloodied, were still fighting on.

It was another victory for Napoleon, a decisive one, but not a crushing one. Casualty figures were similar for both sides, and at the end of Wagram, over 65,000 men had been killed or wounded.

60. PORTLAND WAS THE UNLUCKY PRIME MINISTER

William Henry Cavendish Cavendish-Bentinck, 3rd Duke of Portland, to give him his full name, has a number of claims to fame. Some of them were desirable; some of them weren't. He was the British Prime Minister in 1783 but only served for eight months, making him Britain's shortest ever serving Prime Minister. During his time in office, he signed the Treaty of Paris, in which Britain lost her American colonies at the end of the American Revolution. After a twenty-four year gap, the longest ever between terms of office, he returned to Number 10 in 1807.

On the plus side, he was one of the few men in history who held every noble title: duke, marquess, earl, viscount, and baron. On the down side, two of his own cabinet ministers, Castelreagh and Canning, loathed each other to the point where they fought a duel (neither died), resulting in a scandal that shook the entire government. More pertinent to this fact, however, is that Portland was the Prime Minister who supervised the Fifth Coalition.

After witnessing the dissolution of British rule in America, Portland now watched the Fifth Coalition dissolve when Austria was forced to capitulate, once again, after the Battle of Wagram. His diplomacy and plans were in tatters. Ill health, the stress of the duel and the collapse of the latest coalition led to his resignation early in October of 1809. He died before the end of the month.

61. THOMAS COCHRANE FINISHED NELSON'S JOB

While it is true that the Battle of Trafalgar in 1805 prevented any major challenges to the supremacy of the Royal Navy for over a century, that's not to say there weren't attempts to do just that.

Trafalgar had destroyed a large Franco-Spanish fleet, but not the entire French navy. By 1809, a sizeable force of fifteen French warships had gathered in the Bay of Biscay. The fleet posed a serious threat to shipping: if it broke out into the Atlantic, it could attack merchant shipping or make a dash for the Caribbean, or it could spearhead an invasion of England/Ireland. In short, it was a threat that had to be neutralised.

To prevent the threat from becoming a reality, the Royal Navy had been busy bottling up the French warships. Lord Mulgrave, First Lord of the Admiralty, decided an attack using fire ships would finish them off. With this in mind, he sent a fleet led by Lord Gambier, whose second in command was Thomas Cochrane (Fact 30). The idea was to launch a few old ships stripped of everything valuable (including the crew), filled with flammable substances. These would be ignited and the ships sailed towards enemy shipping, which would either run aground in panic or be set on fire. It was a plan that had previously worked well with tightly packed ships, most famously with the Spanish Armada in the sixteenth century.

Mulgrave should have had concerns because, while it was a plan with precedent, Gambier openly declared it 'a horrible and anti-Christian mode of warfare'. Gambier became even more reticent when Cochrane created several 'explosion ships', fire ships with added barrels of gunpowder, shells, grenades and pretty much every nasty explosive they could get their hands on. The attack was carried out on 11 April, a day that turned out to have perfect weather, according to Cochrane's own diaries, in which he comments that a strong wind was blowing in the right direction.

But there were two problems. Firstly, as Cochrane led his group of fire/explosion ships towards the French, he received no backup from Gambier, who should have led the rest of the fire ships, along with the fleet, which would rain in cannon fire to finish the job. Secondly, one of the fuses on an explosion ship detonated sooner than intended, so the damage it caused was minimal. (Cochrane returned to one of the explosion ships when he realised the ship's dog had been left on board.)

Even with only half the planned ships used in the attack, a third of the French fleet was burnt, sunk or grounded.

Cochrane was a popular hero, but he always riled senior admiralty staff, so Gambier was given the credit even though he had tried to sabotage the attack. The two men constantly argued over who had won the battle, clashing even in the Houses of Parliament. However, the most important outcome was that the French never again dared to raise a fleet against the British.

62. NAPOLEON HAD A SECOND WIFE

Archduchess Maria Ludovica Leopoldina Franziska Therese Josepha Lucia, who, for brevity's sake again, is called Marie-Louise, was the eldest daughter of Frederick II of Austria and his second wife. In 1810, she was nineteen years old; in the same year, Napoleon turned forty. She was Austrian and had grown up at a time when France in general, and Napoleon in particular, were despised. All she had known in her short life was total enmity between Austria and France. However, after the Battle of Wagram in the previous year, Austria had once more been humbled, and Napoleon could do as he pleased.

Napoleon desperately wanted an heir to his imperial title, but Josephine was, by this time, beyond childbearing years. In order to ensure his legacy, Napoleon had to divorce the woman he loved. He then began looking around for a suitable new wife, and Russia seemed an obvious place to look. The agreement after Tilsit meant that the two nations had close connections, and it just so happened that Tsar Alexander's sister was young and available. However, Austria feared such an alliance (it was possible that the offspring of any such union could become both Emperor of France and Tsar of Russia), so as a counter move, Frederick II suggested his daughter, Marie-Louise. There was no regard, whatsoever, for her personal feelings; she was a mere bargaining chip.

When Marie-Louise was told that she was going to marry her country's bitterest enemy, she calmly responded, 'I wish only what my duty commands me to wish.' Royal women of the times were brought up knowing their marriages would probably be arranged according to political expediency.

On 11 March 1810, the archduchess married Napoleon in Vienna ... except he wasn't present. Marie-Louise, who had never met her new husband, instead found her uncle, Archduke Charles, acting as Napoleon's proxy. In just one morning she became Empress of France, Queen of Italy and Madame Bonaparte.

Marie-Louise then set off for France where she finally met her new husband. Almost exactly a year later, she gave birth to their first child, a boy, instantly named Napoleon II, who was also instantly declared King of Rome.

Considering all that was stacked against this marriage, it was a surprisingly loving one. Later on, despite the collapse of Napoleon's fortunes and his abdication in 1814, Marie-Louise was able to keep her imperial rank. She was made the Duchess of Parma in 1815 (a title for life as the coalition did not want her son to use this or any title to try to reclaim the throne). Kept away from her husband in exile, she became the lover of Count von Neipperg, whom she married after Napoleon's death and with whom she had three children. She married again after Neipperg died. Marie-Louise lived in Parma for the rest of her days, but on her death, her body was transferred home to Austria, where she was buried in the imperial crypt in Vienna.

63. A FRENCH PRIVATE CREATED A ROYAL DYNASTY

The title of this fact may lead you to think that it's about Napoleon, but it's actually about the remarkable career and legacy of Jean-Baptiste Bernadotte.

Bernadotte was born in the south of France and joined the army in 1780 at the age of seventeen. During the French Revolutionary War, he was promoted to sergeant, and after that, because the revolutionary leaders were short of good men and Bernadotte was a capable soldier, he rose rapidly through the ranks. He was a colonel by 1792.

Bernadotte continued his military career until, in 1799, while Napoleon was gallivanting around the Middle East, he was made Minister of War. When Napoleon returned and staged the coup that created his consulship, Bernadotte politely refused to get involved, but his reputation was such that Napoleon still gave him an army to lead.

Once Napoleon had crowned himself emperor, he created eighteen marshals of France. These were the most senior generals in the French army, and Bernadotte was one of them. Up until this time, Bernadotte had fought in many battles and many campaigns but none that have echoed down the annals of history. However, he played key roles at Ulm, Austerlitz and Wagram (but was reprimanded for failing to engage at Jena). At Wagram, Bernadotte was forced to retreat with his men, and Napoleon, in one of his legendary rages, stripped him of his command.

But before he had time to feel sorry for himself, Bernadotte was told that he had been elected as the heir presumptive to the Swedish throne (at the time,

Sweden also included Norway). The reasons were somewhat bizarre: the current Swedish King (Charles XIII – definitely an unlucky number for him) had no children, and his wife was beyond her childbearing years. So Charles adopted a Danish prince as his heir, but the prince died just a few months after arriving in Sweden. The country was facing a potential power vacuum. To make matters worse, Sweden was fearful of further war with Russia (they had recently lost Finland to Tsar Alexander) and wanted a capable military man at the head of its government. Why this French marshal? Bernadotte had recently fought a small war with Sweden, and the Swedish prisoners of war felt they had been well treated by him. They believed he was a man of honour.

Bernadotte accepted the title and the position and even changed his name to the much more Swedish sounding Carl John. Following his formal adoption by Charles XIII in 1810, the new Crown Prince became the most popular and powerful man in Sweden. When the king died in 1818, the Crown Prince became Charles XIV (of Sweden) and John III (of Norway). He ruled as a well-regarded monarch until 1844, when he had a stroke on his eighty-first birthday and died a few months later. His family wore the Swedish crown until it was split between Norway and Sweden in the late nineteenth century. The royal House of Bernadotte still rules Sweden today.

64. SPAIN AND BRITAIN FORMED AN ALLIANCE THAT ALMOST WORKED

While there had been a whirlwind of French victories in northern Europe, in the Iberian Peninsula things had not been going so well for the French. The Battle of Corunna had failed to annihilate the British army, and by 1809, Portugal had managed to shrug off French interference. This allowed Arthur Wellesley to link his army of around 20,000 with a Spanish army of some 35,000, led by General Cuesta.

The idea was to use this large Anglo-Spanish force to march on Madrid, which was still stubbornly being held by the French under the leadership (if it could be called that) of Joseph Bonaparte. The allied force met a French army led by Marshal Soult at Talavera, a good few days' march south-west of Madrid. The French had the slightly smaller army (about 45,000), but they were battle-hardened and motivated, something that could not be said for some of the forces on the coalition side.

The Battle of Talavera was fought on 27–28 July 1809, in Spain's baking summer heat. The Spanish held the right flank of the allied formation, which was anchored to the town that gave its name to the battle; the British had the centre and the left. The French, meanwhile, had picked higher ground for their cannon, and it was the French artillery that was to cause Wellesley a large number of casualties over the next two days.

The French tried to grind down the allies with cannon fire, after which the French Dragoons attacked the Spanish, who were then in the process of withdrawing to a better position. What should have been a nuisance that could be repelled turned into a full-blown rout of the Spanish forces. The right flank was littered with rifles, packs and other equipment abandoned by the fleeing soldiers. Adding insult to injury, the panicked troops then, shamelessly, raided the British baggage at the rear. While many Spanish soldiers returned the next day, hundreds just melted away, never to play a role in the battle again.

Wellesley neutralised the accurate French cannon fire by keeping his soldiers on the rear slopes of hills and ridges, ordering them to rise up and attack the French as they advanced. British volley fire and, in one case, bayonet charges broke the French forces. By the evening of the 28th, the French had no choice but to retreat. A fire broke out in the dried grass, burning many of the wounded left on the battlefield. Losses were roughly equal; however, on the coalition side, the British suffered far more casualties, which meant Wellesley had lost about a quarter of his force. In a way, this was a rerun of Corunna; by the end of the battle, the French had clearly lost, but the strategic situation was still with France. Wellesley's forces were in no shape to take Madrid, the main objective of the campaign, but a battle had been won, nonetheless.

65. L'Arc de Triomphe Is Not Only for Napoleon

L'Arc de Triomphe de l'Étoile is the greatest triumphal arch in the world and a landmark Paris monument. It was commissioned by Napoleon in 1806 and was designed specifically to commemorate his victory at Austerlitz.

The architect was Jean Chalgrin, who created a neoclassical version of the ancient Roman triumphal arches built to honour great imperial victories of the past. Chalgrin (encouraged by Napoleon) took the idea and inflated it. For example, one of the few remaining original triumphal arches was erected for Titus in Rome, and that is about 15 metres high. L'Arc de Triomphe, by comparison, is 50 metres high.

The monument was intended to dominate the skyline, and by placing it in the centre of a roundabout with twelve roads emanating from it, it looks as if all roads lead not to Rome but to the arch itself. L'Arc de Triomphe is Napoleon's hubris built in stone.

An ambitious project of this size took time to construct, so when Napoleon triumphantly arrived back in Paris in 1810, a wooden version was erected over the unfinished structure. Chalgrin died in 1811. After this, Napoleon's political and military fortunes began to wane, so neither Chalgrin nor Napoleon ever saw it completed.

Finally finished in 1836, the arch was further adapted after the First World War to accommodate France's Tomb of the Unknown Soldier. Its eternal flame is said to be the inspiration for the one on US President Kennedy's tomb.

66. Napoleon Was the Ultimate Nepotist

Although Napoleon became a great general and a powerful emperor, it should not be forgotten that he had grown up in a large and only modestly wealthy family in a backwater of Europe. For all his achievements and arrogance, he was a remarkably loyal man, particularly with regard to his immediate family. His actions often seem contradictory because he was a meritocratic general who rewarded results above all else. On the battlefield, background didn't matter; those who performed well could expect to be rewarded. But in the realms of politics and governance, he was possibly the ultimate nepotist.

Napoleon was close to his family, and as his power grew, he genuinely wanted to share it with his loved ones. Whether they were able to act as capable rulers is another matter entirely, but handing out countries the way most people hand out sweets shows a failure to understand the possible consequences of misrule.

The oldest surviving Bonaparte sibling was Joseph. Napoleon made him King of Naples (1806–08), where he ruled inefficiently until he got a promotion and was made King of Spain (he was replaced in Naples by General Murat). He was so unsuccessful a ruler during the Peninsular War that he survived only because he had been propped up by the French military until he abdicated in 1813.

Napoleon's younger brother got to be King of Holland in 1806–10. As a thank you to his elder brother, Louis named two of his three sons Napoleon. As was the case with all of Napoleon's family members, when his power faded, so did theirs. However, Louis' youngest son would grow up to become Napoleon III.

At the age of twenty-three, the youngest brother, Jerome, was granted the title of King of Westphalia (an area in modern day Germany) in 1807. He was out of a job by 1813.

The sisters were similarly ennobled: Elisa positively collected titles and became Princess of Lucca and Piombino, Grand Duchess of Tuscany and Countess of Compignano. She was the most politically active of the sisters and was a supporter of the arts.

Pauline was Napoleon's favourite sister. Beautiful and promiscuous, she was the subject of many scandals, but Napoleon made her a Princess of France, and in later life she married and became Princess Consort of Sulmona and of Rossano. Pauline was the only sibling to follow Napoleon into his Elba exile.

Caroline, the youngest of Napoleon's sisters, married General Murat, so that made her Queen of Naples until 1815.

Napoleon's mother was treated to every luxury and was granted the title of Mother of his Imperial Majesty the Emperor.

Lucien Bonaparte was the exception to Napoleon's generosity towards family. The brothers did not get along, and after going into self-imposed exile, Lucien returned to France only after Napoleon had abdicated. Unlike his siblings, who had hitched rides on Napoleon's star, Lucien had made a wise decision to stay away; he became Prince of Canino in 1814–40, well after his other siblings' elevations had passed into history.

67. Wellington Made a Pact with the Devil

On 27 September 1810, Wellington, leading an Anglo-Portuguese army of 50,000, met Marshals Ney and Masséna at the Battle of Bussaco. Once again Wellington showed his tactical ability as he sheltered his main force on the reverse slope of ridges to protect it from French cannon fire and to obscure his troops' movements. These tactics neutralised French numerical superiority, and a brilliant victory forced the French to retreat.

The battle was, in many ways, a great relief because for months Wellington had sat silent in Portugal, apparently doing nothing. His reports were so dull and so lacking in any interest in attacking the French that he was very nearly removed from his position as commander. It was only the fact that his brother Richard was in government that kept his post secure.

The reason for Wellington's inactivity was revealed when, apparently from nowhere, French manoeuvres were blocked by a colossal and previously unknown series of walls, blockhouses and forts. Masséna demanded an explanation as to why no one knew anything about this chain of fortifications, to which he got the response, 'Wellington has made them.' Masséna replied, 'Only the devil could have made them.'

It turned out that far from sitting idle, Wellington had been busy constructing his fortifications but was concerned that if he mentioned them in dispatches back to Britain, the surprise might well have been picked up by French spies. Wellington was very good at keeping secrets, as he once said, 'Be discreet in all things, and so render it unnecessary to be mysterious about any.'

The Lines of Torres Vedras were not a solid wall but a series of walls linked to areas with troop concentrations and forts positioned in highly defendable areas like the tops of hills. Three layers of defensive lines had been built. They were designed to stop any attempts by the French to push through to Lisbon.

Masséna attempted an assault in mid-October, but after two days of heavy fighting, no breach had been made. The French could not break the line. Meanwhile, Wellington had prepared another nasty surprise: he had carried out a scorched earth policy in the area beyond the fortifications. Armies at this time lived off the land, so with no food in the nearby area, Masséna and Ney either had to stay and starve or retreat to a better provisioned area. The French remained in the shadow of the walls for some time before illness and malnutrition began to set in.

The French had no option but to retreat. Wellington's meticulous planning had ensured Portugal was no longer under threat of invasion. The French had started out with the much larger army of 65,000 men; however, by the time the French returned to Spain, their troop numbers had dwindled to around 40,000. Wellington had won not just a campaign that saved Portugal, he had also shattered a French army, the first general to do so in the era of Napoleon's dominance.

68. The War of 1812 Has Been Forgotten

The War of 1812 tends to be ignored by both sides in the conflict. In America, the war gets lost because it is sandwiched between two far more important wars: the American Revolution and the American Civil War. In Britain, it's overlooked because the far more important wars with Napoleon were going on at the same time.

The causes of the war were several and included British attempts to blockade American trade by attacking American shipping (brought about by Britain's war with France), pressganging Americans in ports and forcing them to serve on Royal Navy ships (the Brits needed more men to fight Napoleon) and American resentment of British support for Native Americans, who were under attack by expansionist America. Because Britain was fully occupied fighting Napoleon, it didn't want a war with America; nevertheless, the Americans felt provoked. Further, there had to be a consideration by the Americans that by fighting Britain at this time, they might get a better deal from their ex-colonial overlord when it was reeling from a much more dangerous foe.

That last point is conjecture but not an unreasonable assumption. Either way, President James Madison declared war on Britain in June 1812 – and almost immediately regretted it. In order to strike the first blow, US troops attempted an invasion of Canada, then a British colony (the only time the two countries have been officially at war), but were defeated by the Canadian militia.

All the early land battles were fought by proxies for the British (although the Royal Navy did fight on the Atlantic and Great Lakes), who had to depend on small garrison forces in Canada, militias and Native American allies. They all surprised everyone by acquitting themselves far better than had been expected. So, while Madison had counted on an expansionist war, he wasn't increasing American territory.

It took the defeat of Napoleon in 1814 for the British to release a large number of troops to enter the fray, and even then their main invasion force numbered less than 5,000, showing that this war was of little importance to the British. In 1814, the Americans lost the Battle of Baldensburg, leaving the road to the capital open. President Madison and his government fled, and British troops swarmed into Washington D. C., where they set fire to government buildings including the Capitol and the White House (which was later painted white to hide the smoke and fire damage). This was intended as a lesson to Madison to show how badly he had miscalculated the war.

The Battle of Baltimore followed shortly and resulted in the defeat of the British, after which they moved for an armistice. The shipping blockade and the cost of the war meant that America was almost bankrupt. The Treaty of Ghent changed little as there were no territorial gains for either side. The problem of impressment was no longer relevant as the Napoleonic Wars were over, but Britain did agree to abandon its support for the Native Americans.

69. Robert Jenkinson Is the Greatest Unknown Prime Minister

While France was being ruled by one man as emperor, Britain was a democracy. The term must be used with caution. In the nineteenth century it certainly wasn't a democracy in the modern sense. Women couldn't vote, neither could men without land, and voting was done in public so the MP could 'check' you were voting correctly. But as imperfect as it was, it was more adaptable than an absolute monarchy.

This was fortunate because, as previously discussed (Fact 3), the British King George III was mad for most of his reign. His inability to rule effectively would have been a disaster for any country at war. As it was, the primary responsibility for the governance of Britain fell to the Members of Parliament, who varied greatly in ability but could be changed regularly and painlessly if necessary.

In 1812, however, the new Prime Minister came to power in a most unexpected way. On the evening of 11 May, then Prime Minster Spencer Perceval walked into the lobby of the House of Commons and was shot. The assassin was not a French spy or an Irish nationalist or a home-grown anarchist, but a disgruntled constituent called John Bellingham, who had had his petitions turned down (there has to be a lesson in this for all politicians). The single shot turned out to be fatal, and Perceval's rather average career is now remembered because he is the only British Prime Minister to have ever been assassinated.

Perceval's replacement was Robert Jenkinson, the 2nd Earl of Liverpool, who was previously the Secretary of State for War and the Colonies. In that post he had defied popular opinion among cabinet colleagues to support Wellington's maintenance of what was then a small force in Portugal. That force grew and won eventual victory over France in the Peninsular War.

Liverpool was to supervise British contributions to the wars against Napoleon, but he also had to worry about war with America. In both conflicts he was at the forefront of the negotiations for settlements, and in both cases, rather than itching for more conflict, he showed willingness to compromise for the sake of peace, demonstrating pragmatism and a desire for calm.

Liverpool was also Prime Minister during the infamous 'Peterloo Massacre' of 1819, when a peaceful demonstration for parliamentary reform resulted in the deaths of fifteen civilians whose leaders were tried for sedition.

Lord Liverpool was to remain Prime Minister until 1827, making him one of the longest serving Prime Ministers in British history and a pivotal figure of the early nineteenth century. During his eventful time in office, his deeds were often overshadowed by the martial prowess of the Duke of Wellington and the total excesses of the Prince Regent. But he guided his country through two major foreign wars and turbulent times at home, events that affected millions of lives. Given his role and influences, it is difficult to understand just why he slid into obscurity.

70. Forlorn Hope Won a Bloody Siege

Badajoz is in the west of Spain near the Portuguese border. In 1812, the main route of travel and communication from Lisbon to the Spanish interior was controlled by this walled city. Behind its formidable, state-of-the-art defences was a garrison of 4,700 French troops.

Wellington arrived at the town in the middle of March with an Anglo-Portuguese army of 27,000, but even though he outnumbered the garrison by nearly six to one, the defences of Badajoz were so well designed that it had already resisted two previous sieges. A swift assault was impossible.

Anticipating this, Wellington had brought with him dozens of cannon to soften up the walls. These included heavy howitzers, which blasted shells over the fortifications to pound the garrison and townsfolk. After nearly three weeks of bombardment from over fifty pieces of artillery, three gaps had been created in the outer wall of the city. These breaches were large enough to allow an assault. The timing was perfect because Wellington had received word that French Marshall Soult was on his way with a relief force. It was now or never.

On the night of 6 April, Wellington ordered an attack. The first troops were volunteers known as the 'Forlorn Hope' because the casualty numbers in the first wave of sieges were usually over 90 per cent. The first to attack were committing themselves to probable suicide, but as there were tempting rewards for the survivors, there was often competition for a place. As well as cash gifts, automatic promotions were guaranteed, and there was the likelihood of a mention in dispatches, a huge career boost for junior officers.

While it was hoped the initial advance might go unnoticed under the cover of night, a French sentry spotted the Forlorn Hope, and as it reached one of the breaches, it was met with point blank volley fire from French muskets. Wellington had no choice. He was committed to the assault, so thousands of men were thrown at the gaps in the hope that the sheer force of numbers would overwhelm the defenders. The French, in turn, had prepared all kinds of nasty surprises: as well as musket fire, masonry and rocks were hurled from above, as were barrels of gunpowder set with fuses and even burning bales of hay.

The attackers were being slaughtered, but as soon as one man fell, another took his place. The breech was beginning to fill with dead Portuguese and British soldiers, forcing other soldiers to struggle over their dead or dying comrades. The fighting lasted a few short hours, but once Wellington's troops were into the town, the French commander realised further resistance was futile, and he surrendered.

But it was the early stages of the assault that had shocked everyone. In the aftermath it was said that blood ran like rivers into the trenches, and in those few short hours, Wellington had suffered more than 4,800 casualties. It was a victory for Wellington, but one that came at a high price.

71. NAPOLEON'S RUSSIAN INVASION STARTED WELL

While Wellington was slogging his way through Spain, Napoleon was amassing a colossal force for his invasion of Russia. He had put together an army of around 500,000 (as always, the exact numbers are endlessly debated by historians), with nearly 300,000 of these constituting the main fighting force. It was less an army and more an unstoppable force, designed to crush Russian power, just as he had crushed all the other major continental powers.

Napoleon understood the importance of stores and provisions and ensured that that his army would be well supplied. Along with a huge baggage train, 6,000 carts and wagons travelled with the troops and were themselves supported by a system of supply dumps near the Russian front.

The French invasion of Russia, known in Russia as the Patriotic War of 1812, began on 21 June, when Napoleon crossed the Niemen River into Russian Poland. At first there were only a few minor skirmishes, mainly at Vilnius, but the Russian forces couldn't make a dent in an opposing force of this size, so Napoleon and his Grande Armée marched ominously eastwards.

It is wrong to think of this army as one immensely long column of troops. Napoleon split this force among his marshals and allowed them to lead different army groups, separate from and independent of each other. Consequently, there was never a battle in this campaign where Napoleon had all his troops fighting on the same field of battle at the same time.

The first real test for Napoleon came two months into the campaign in mid-August, when the Russians, under General Tolly, finally decided to resist. Napoleon wanted to capture the walled city of Smolensk, and the Russians weren't going to allow this without a fight. Realising that the city was both well defended and heavily garrisoned, Napoleon used more than 200 artillery pieces to blast away at the walls in order to create a breach as quickly as possible. His tactics were a little too successful as the city was set on fire. Tolly ordered the evacuation of his forces and destroyed all the arms dumps and food stores to deprive Napoleon of any practical gains. When victory was his, Napoleon realised that he had conquered a city reduced to a smouldering ruin – a city of no real value.

The Battle of Smolensk was, in many ways, to set the tone for Napoleon's campaigns in Russia. On one hand, he was winning; on the other, none of his conquests were particularly spectacular or strategically important. His victories were feeling a little on the hollow side. By now, despite the huge baggage train and supply dumps, food was starting to run low. True, Smolensk was over 530 miles to the east of Warsaw, which showed a huge gain in territory, but the main Russian army had yet to be defeated. Supplies were thin on the ground, and Moscow was still another 240 miles further east.

72. THE BATTLE OF SALAMANCA OPENED THE ROAD TO MADRID

After Badajoz (Fact 70), Wellington marched all over Spain. By now he had an army of around 50,000, a largely Anglo-Portuguese force with some Spanish regulars. The increasing size of the allied army was echoed by the French forces under General Marmont, who had done an excellent job of mirroring Wellington's movements and preventing him from getting close to Madrid ... so far.

On 22 July 1812, Wellington observed that the French army appeared ready to give battle, but he noted that the French had separated their left flank from their main body of troops, a tactical error he could use to his advantage. So, although he was facing a force of roughly equal size on ground chosen by the enemy, Wellington engaged, sending in infantry to attack the French left flank. The initial attack was repulsed, but a subsequent bayonet charge pushed home the advantage.

When the French saw the British Dragoons (heavy cavalry) slowly advancing, their troops reformed into anti-cavalry squares. This would have been a sensible decision had it not been for the fact that the soldiers still faced British infantry, and the squares were a poor formation for dealing with the continuing infantry attack.

As it was, by the time the Dragoons arrived, the French flank had broken and run. A rout was averted but only after considerable losses. It was during the chaos that Marmont was hit by shrapnel and badly wounded, as was his deputy. With the foremost commanders now out of action, the reigns of command were taken up by General Clausel, who had been third in command.

Following the shattering of the French left flank, Clausel attacked the centre of Wellington's forces, hoping to relieve the pressure on his own troops. The initial onslaught worked but was ultimately absorbed by Anglo-Portuguese troops. While Marmont and his deputy returned to France to recover from their wounds, fierce fighting continued, but it was turning into a rearguard action, which allowed the bulk of the French forces to escape. Spanish troops took no part in the battle as they had been positioned to block French escape routes.

Although a major part of the French army managed to extricate itself from the battle, it was a damaging defeat for the French and a decisive victory for Wellington. Of the 50,000 French troops, 6,000 were dead or wounded, and another 7,000 had been captured. To the military historians who portray Wellington as cautious and defensive, the Battle of Salamanca is the exception they have to concede. This was a clear case of bold and aggressive tactics used to win the day and seal a major victory that opened the road to Madrid. It was the battle that established Wellington as an offensive general.

Wellington was to remain in Madrid for two months (forcing Joseph Bonaparte, the supposed King of Spain, to flee). Even then, he left only when returning French forces threatened his communication lines with Portugal.

73. THE FRENCH FINALLY MET THE RUSSIANS AT BORODINO

When Napoleon planned his invasion of Russia, he had never specifically targeted Moscow. His ultimate goal was to fight and destroy the Russian army to ensure Tsar Alexander I's complete capitulation to his will. By September, three months into the campaign, the Russian army had yet to show itself in full force, and Napoleon was drawn further and further towards Russia's distant capital.

In early September, near the small town of Borodino on the banks of the Moskva River, Napoleon finally met the Russian army of over 120,000 men, supported by more than 600 cannon dug into trenches and earthworks. Napoleon sensed his moment had come and addressed his troops: 'The battle of Borodino is the most glorious, most difficult, and most creditable operation of war carried out by Gauls.'

Contrary to the content of his rousing speech, about half of Napoleon's army wasn't French, and, furthermore, the battle turned out to be one of his least imaginative. It started at dawn on 7 September, with 100 French cannon softening up the Russian front lines. Then Generals Ney and de Beauharnais (Josephine's son) moved into action. The Russians responded with a flanking cavalry attack, which neutralised the French assault.

On this occasion, Napoleon was unusually far from the action, and so his orders were slow to respond to a changing situation. In fact, he seemed sluggish and cautious throughout the day's events. Some historians think that the more troops Napoleon commanded the less effective he became. Certainly Borodino was no Austerlitz or Marengo, so it's a valid observation. However, it's also worth remembering that Napoleon had been vigorously campaigning for the best part of fifteen years, and the young officer was now an overweight, middle-aged man. He simply didn't have the same energy as before, and Borodino may have been a reflection of this. There is also evidence that he was ill at the time of the battle.

A further reason for the sheer bloodiness of the day's combat was that the Russians were used to fighting the Ottomans, who rarely gave quarter or, indeed, took prisoners. As such, the Russians fought tenaciously, and when other armies would have surrendered, they fought on even when the situation was hopeless. Napoleon said of the Russian soldiers, 'They are citadels that have to be demolished with cannon.'

Eventually the Russians broke, but Napoleon failed to use his usual energetic tactics and remained on the field of battle, rather than sending in reserves to harass and shatter the retreating Russian army. As his goal was to strip Russia of its effective fighting ability, this failure to give chase turned a potential strategic victory into a merely tactical one.

Napoleon had lost over 30,000 troops and the Russians lost over 40,000, but the Russians were in retreat. Borodino was a French victory, if an unconvincing one. Nevertheless, Moscow was now only 70 miles away, and with no effective resistance between Napoleon and the Russian capital, Moscow was looking vulnerable.

74. The Russians Destroyed Their Own Capital

A week after the Battle of Borodino, Napoleon entered Moscow on 14 September 1812. Just getting there was a staggering achievement in itself. No western general had ever before been able to reach so far into the Russian interior (although the city had previously fallen to eastern warlords) – and none has done so since.

Moscow itself was largely bare and unoccupied; once again Napoleon found a city emptied of food and supplies. His army may have found good winter quarters, but it also faced possible starvation. Under any other circumstances, the capture of a nation's capital would result in negotiations for the surrender of the defeated power; however, to Napoleon's surprise, neither Tsar Alexander I nor anyone representing him was waiting. Instead, Napoleon was given the keys to the city and allowed to settle down in the Kremlin.

As the French moved in, Russians who had not already done so were moving out, including Governor Count Rostopchin. It was Rostopchin who showed how brutally pragmatic Russians can be when he deliberately ordered the burning of Moscow. Some fires had already broken out as the Grande Armée marched in, but these isolated acts of arson were turned into an inferno by Russian saboteurs.

By the end of September, despite French attempts to round up and shoot arsonists, Moscow had been turned into a burnt ruin. By 18–19 October, Napoleon had no option but to order a general retreat. Winter was coming, and it was already starting to snow.

75. THE RUSSIANS HAD AN ALLY IN THE WEATHER

With Moscow a burnt husk, the Russians had forced Napoleon and his once Grande Armée to leave what they had planned to be their winter quarters and move out onto the Russian steppes. So far in the Russian campaign, the Russian generals had proved to be mediocre. They had been very effective at using Russia's colossal size to absorb the shock of Napoleon's invasion, but when it came to actual combat, they had yet to land a serious blow ... that is, until 'General Winter' came along.

Along with the myth that Napoleon invaded the country in one huge column, there is another that the Russians left the defeat of Napoleon up to the winter. This is not entirely true. The Russians secured a minor victory at the Battle of Tarutino and suffered a defeat at Maloyaroslavets. However, the Russian army showed its military failings by being unable to land a killer blow, even when Napoleon was leading the retreat of a cold and hungry army. Napoleon, meanwhile, continued to hope that one of these engagements would result in the decisive victory that would bring Tsar Alexander to the negotiating table. Instead, he was forced to continue his retreat through the thickening winter blizzards.

Military historians regularly make reference to 'dangerously stretched supply lines' or 'over extending', and it's not always clear what the repercussions of these can mean. While the results are sometimes overstated, in this instance, it would be hard to exaggerate the devastation.

Between them, hypothermia and starvation killed more of Napoleon's men than the Russians ever did.

His troops had little in the way of warm clothing and, therefore, little protection against the extreme cold. As they trudged on, the lack of grass meant the starving horses were slaughtered and used to feed the famished troops ... which meant that Napoleon was now without cavalry. When, in early December, Napoleon learned that there had been an attempted coup against him in France, he seized a sledge to rush ahead of his freezing, starving army so as to get back to his empire before any further political damage could be done. Unforgivably, he abandoned his troops in order to put out his version of events before it was generally realised that his Russian campaign had ended in humiliating defeat and a colossal loss of life.

Only 22,000 French troops returned to the initial staging post at Vilnius, which would imply that more than 400,000 had died, but not all those who left from Vilnius had gone on to Moscow. The Prussian and Austrian contingents were never fanatical supporters and, as such, melted away back to their homelands. It is also thought that of the 80,000–100,000 French soldiers who retreated from Moscow and were left to fend for themselves, many changed their names and blended into the local population. Even taking these mitigating factors into consideration, Russia had managed to destroy the largest army ever seen in Europe. Napoleon had been humbled; the sharks were circling.

76. A BATTLE WAS FOUGHT AFTER THE PEACE TREATY HAD BEEN SIGNED

While Napoleon was invading Russia, the War of 1812 (Fact 68) was already under way in America and included many actions that took place in 1813 and 1814. By and large, the British, with their Native American and Canadian allies, won a lot more engagements than they lost, eventually forcing the Americans to the negotiating table.

While the American Revolution was still within living memory, Britain had no appetite to rerun the fight for independence, especially at the same time as it was fighting Napoleon. Instead, the diplomatic wrangling over what a peace settlement should look like was carried out between two mutually acknowledged nation states.

Britain had plenty to bargain with; its territorial gains to America's detriment had been significant. Maine, for example, was then largely under British control. The British had earlier pushed for a Native American state to act as a buffer between British-held territory and America, but the United States would not agree. This is one of the great 'what ifs' of history. American history would have been very different if an area like Maine had become a separate nation for the native peoples whose borders would have been guaranteed by the British Empire. But it wasn't to be.

Although the war itself is little remembered, most Americans know that one of its battles inspired the poem that would eventually become America's national anthem, 'The Star Spangled Banner'.

Most of the peace talks were carried out in the neutral territory of Belgium, and eventually, in December of

1814 (showing how the official name of the war is just plain wrong), with a few concessions, the final agreement was a return to the status quo, with things more or less the same as before the war. The terms were ratified in the Treaty of Ghent.

Ghent is, however, a long way from New Orleans, and it was at that city where a bloody and completely pointless battle was fought. The day before the treaty was signed, a British force of 11,000 arrived at New Orleans. The defence of the city was led by Andrew Jackson, who would go on to become the seventh President of the United States. He attacked the British on the night of 23 December but failed to remove them after their surprise assault was bloodily repelled.

For the next week or so, the two armies exchanged artillery fire, the Americans trying to break up the larger British force and the British trying to grind down the defences. Neither side knew that peace had already been declared.

On 9 January 1815, Sir Edward Packenham ordered a two-pronged assault. While there was some clever use of artillery and even rocket support, Packenham ordered his troops to attack the strongest part of the American defence. By the end of the day, the British had suffered over 2,000 casualties (including Packenham, who died in battle) to Jackson's seventy-one. It was America's biggest victory in this conflict, so it was a shame that the war had actually ended.

77. A Sixth Coalition Couldn't Hurt

In the summer of 1812, Napoleon had mustered the Grande Armée and had invaded Russia. This activated a number of treaties and triggered a flurry of alliances and diplomatic communications. One particularly galling clause from the Treaty of Tilsit was that Prussia had to support Napoleon in any such military endeavours. This was simply unacceptable to thousands of Prussian soldiers and officers, many of whom deserted Napoleon's cause and some of whom would join the Russian forces.

Following Tilsit and with an army in the area, Napoleon attacked Sweden for dragging its heels on joining the unpopular and inefficient Continental System (Fact 52). He humiliated Sweden by confiscating Pomerania, an area in modern-day Germany, which then had been under Swedish control for 200 years.

Britain had continued to fight France, largely in Spain and Portugal, and was all too willing to assist in creating another coalition against Napoleon. By December 1812, Britain might have been winning in both the Iberian Peninsula and America, but it needed all the help it could get on the continent.

The Sixth Coalition (1812–14) brought together all of the European nations which had had enough of France and its emperor. After the disastrous French invasion of Russia, Russia joined Prussia, Austria, Portugal, Spain, Sweden, some German states and the United Kingdom in a determined effort to halt and defeat Napoleon.

Napoleon, however, was not fighting alone; his Grande Armée was nearly 700,000 strong, and only about half of it was French. His military resources were bolstered with forces from Italy, the Duchy of Warsaw (which Napoleon had created) and a large swathe of German states called the Confederation of the Rhine. While America was never officially involved in these wars or aligned to Napoleon, US troops and the American navy were frequent thorns in the side of the British throughout this era.

By the end of 1813, when Napoleon had suffered a number of key defeats, the allies presented him with the Frankfurt Proposals. These stated that Napoleon would remain in power in France but that France was to return to her 'natural borders'. Under the circumstances, it was a pretty good deal. It showed that after all the years of French aggression, Europe wanted a return to peace more than it wanted to crush or humiliate France and its emperor. What was surprising was that all of this was Austria's idea. Of all the territories in Europe, Austria would probably be the most justified in seeking revenge.

It was Metternich, however, who coaxed the other allies to offer favourable terms in an attempt to end the fighting, once and for all. But Napoleon delayed. He still believed he could defeat the armies allied against him. By the time they invaded France in 1814, the favourable terms had been withdrawn. Napoleon tried to negotiate peace based on the proposals, but it was too late. The opportunity had gone.

78. Spain Collapsed at Vitoria

While the winter of 1812 had been brutal for Napoleon, it had been a period of reorganisation for Wellington, which enabled his swift advances in the spring and summer of 1813. Wellington's goal was to use this campaigning season to finally neutralise French authority in Spain. He got his chance at Vitoria in June, when his Anglo-Portuguese (and Spanish) army of 80,000 met the remaining French army of 60,000.

Wellington had more troops, their morale was high and, unknown to him, his opponent General Jourdan (Facts 10 and 13) was ill with a fever. Wellington had every advantage and he used it. The ensuing battle proved that Wellington did not just anchor his forces to a terrain feature, absorb cannon fire and counterattack; this battle was all about manoeuvrability.

Much of the fighting was on and around the bridges of the Zadorra River, which flowed past the city of Vitoria, at this time clogged up with Joseph Bonaparte's huge baggage train. Using the situation to their advantage, the allies moved both north and south of the meandering bends of the river. When Jourdan's illness led to sluggish responses, it became apparent that the French faced potential envelopment.

To prevent this from happening, Jourdan ordered a counterattack supported by furious cannon fire from some forty artillery pieces. This, plus the bitter fighting around one of the bridges, resulted in most of the allied casualties.

The French artillery held several areas of high ground, which commanded much of the river valley. The British captured the hill of Arinez early on, and towards the end of the fighting, when the French artillery made a final stand at Zuazo Ridge, it was taken by British forces in a direct assault.

The day had not started well for the French, and at no point in the battle did Jourdan ever look like he was going to overcome Wellington. By late afternoon the French were in full retreat. A rear guard ensured tens of thousands of French soldiers escaped capture, but that only mitigated what was a crushing defeat. While casualty numbers were roughly equal (a little over 5,000 each), Wellington could afford the losses, whereas the French could not. The French also lost all of their 150 artillery pieces and the whole of Joseph's baggage train, groaning under the weight of treasures plundered from the Spanish crown. This booty saved the French from pursuit by the British when order broke down as soldiers began to loot the rich pickings. Wellington disgusted by this said, 'We have in the service the scum of the earth as common soldiers.'

Vitoria was a fitting close to the Peninsular War. It had taken years, but the French finally had been ejected from the Iberian Peninsula, thanks largely to the highly effective leadership of Arthur Wellesley. After this, he marched north with his force, and as the allies vied with each other to reach the border first, Wellington won by crossing into the south of France in December of 1813.

79. THE NAPOLEONIC CODE IS AN ENDURING LEGACY

Napoleon was not just a general and an emperor; he was a law maker too. Today in France, there are more than sixty 'codes' of law that are the foundation of France's legal system. These can be traced back to 1804 and the *Code civil des Français*, forever remembered as the Napoleonic Code. This wasn't the first modern legal code, but as his power grew over Europe, it became the first to have a pancontinental scope, rather than just a national one. It was the main judicial code throughout Napoleon's rule over most of continental Europe.

Its influence has been, in some ways, greater than Napoleon's military legacy as it enshrined freedom of religion, stopped privileges based on hereditary titles, determined that government jobs should be awarded on the basis of merit and protected property rights ... all under the law. None of these ideas were new, but to have them all encompassed in a legal code that crossed borders, languages and cultures was ground-breaking. Their impact and importance are the reasons why they outlasted Napoleon's reign.

There is a long list of countries that have chosen to use the Napoleonic Code as a basis for their prevailing laws. While it may be unsurprising that places like Italy or Poland (until the end of the Second World War) chose to do so, the laws of more exotic places such as Romania, Egypt and Chile are also based on this revolutionary code.

80. THE BATTLE OF THE NATIONS WAS BIG AND BLOODY

In early 1813, Napoleon rebuilt his army and knew that he must cow at least one of the major powers to get a peace treaty and much-needed breathing space. On one hand, this tenacity is to be admired; on the other, shrugging off the deaths of tens of thousands, only to fight more battles, explains why it is estimated that this twenty-five year period saw roughly 6 million deaths.

During the summer of 1813, Napoleon tore into German territory with a string of victories. However, a Swedish-Prussian alliance at the Battle of Großbeeren stopped the French from taking Berlin. This forced Napoleon to centre his forces on Leipzig, where he faced the combined might of Russia, Prussia, Sweden and Austria.

The numbers are staggering. In the era of the musket, Napoleon amassed an army of 225,000, with 700 artillery pieces. The French were supported by contingents from Poland, Italy and some German states, altogether a mighty army that would have overwhelmed any normal force. But Napoleon had stirred up a hornet's nest, and he now faced virtually the rest of continental Europe's combined might, amounting to more than 380,000 soldiers, supported by some 1,500 cannon.

The three-day battle at Leipzig has become known as the Battle of the Nations as over half a million men, representing nearly a dozen different territories, clashed in epic conflict. As Wellington was otherwise occupied in Spain, Britain was the only major power not present.

Because Napoleon had lost most of his veteran forces in his Russian campaign, for the first time ever, most of his forces were unproven new recruits. There had been huge resentment in France as, one more time, Napoleon drained the reserves of young men to fight for his glory. By comparison, he faced many troops that had not only fought in previous campaigns but also had every motivation to end French aggression, once and for all.

The rivers that ran through the Leipzig area broke the allied forces into smaller groups, and Napoleon planned to attack each of them in turn. This could have worked because, while Napoleon could do as he alone wanted, the coalition had to deal with the vying egos of different monarchs.

Day one (16 October) saw the lack of a cohesive allied strategy result in failed offensives, but their sheer numbers stopped Napoleon from breaking through. Day two was relatively quiet, although Bernadotte (Fact 63), once one of Napoleon's most trusted generals, arrived as 'Prince Carl' with Swedish reinforcements to fight for the allies. On the third day, Napoleon's German allies defected, and there were further attempts to encircle the emperor, which encouraged him to try to sue for peace. And so, on the fourth and final day of battle, Napoleon suffered the most decisive defeat of his career in a battle that was the bloodiest (some 100,000 casualties) of the Napoleonic Wars. It was the biggest battle in history until the First World War.

81. Capitulation Was Not in Napoleon's Repertoire

With both 1812 and 1813 ending in humiliating defeats for Napoleon, 1814 was looking like the year of final capitulation. Prior to Leipzig he had been offered favourable terms in the Frankfurt Proposals, which allowed France to keep some of its conquered territory and Napoleon to remain as emperor. However, Napoleon pretended that the Battle of Nations hadn't happened as he cast around for agreement on those original terms. But things had changed: the allies had just won a major victory, and Napoleon had lost two major armies in as many years. The allies wanted a new set of terms.

All things considered, the revised offer was still very generous. True, Napoleon would have to relinquish Belgium, but at least he could continue to rule France as emperor. The British, however, did not support such favourable terms and wanted Napoleon to abdicate. This was hardly surprising because, while Austria wanted a strong France to act as a counter balance to Russia (a rising military power), Britain recognised (correctly) that as long as Napoleon was in power, he would keep trying his luck with aggressive military campaigns.

As the allies closed in on Napoleon, who was based in Paris, it seemed as if he had nothing left to do but surrender. However, capitulation was simply not in Napoleon's repertoire, and so, with his remaining (but sizeable) force of around 60,000, he attempted to take on Prussia and Russia in February of 1814.

In the space of five days (although this is called the Six Day Campaign), he fought four battles. While none was the size of Borodino or Austerlitz, they still showed, even then, what Napoleon could do. He won every single engagement.

The last of these battles was fought on Valentine's Day and is known as the Battle of Vauchamps. Here Napoleon, with just 10,000 soldiers, took on a Prussian force of 21,000, led by Field Marshal Blücher (Fact 89). After the initial skirmishes, it was French Marshal Grouchy's cavalry that did the most damage as it ceaselessly harassed the retreating Prussian forces, even breaking several anti-cavalry squares. Having lost more than a third of his men, Blücher had to conduct a forced night march just to get his remaining troops out of harm's way.

The actions in February of 1814 can be compared to those of a cornered animal which lashes out while knowing the game is over. Vauchamps simply reminded everyone how dangerous Napoleon was with an army, but none of his final victories were significant enough to stop the inevitable. After a few more minor engagements, the battle for Paris was won, and the Austrian army was the first to enter the city in March of 1814. On 2 April, the French Senate voted to depose Napoleon. When he ordered his generals to attack the capital on 4 April, they mutinied. The War of the Sixth Coalition ended with the abdication and exile of Emperor Napoleon. It was game over for the Corsican.

82. Mrs Arbuthnot Knew It All

The story of this era is heaving with generals, royalty and politicians. With the exception of some wives and lovers, there are few women who make it into the story of the Napoleonic Wars. However, there is one who was neither a member of a royal family nor the lover of a key figure: her name is Harriet Fane.

Harriet came from a minor aristocratic background and married MP Charles Arbuthnot in 1814. He was twenty-six years her senior. Charles was never a major player in the political arena, but he was Ambassador to the Ottoman Empire and later became the First Commissioner of Woods and Forests, hardly an earth-shattering role. However, for the new Mrs Arbuthnot, her marriage gave her access to the great men of the times, many of whom would become close friends.

Harriet was a political hostess for the Tory party and an obsessive diarist who recorded details of meetings, conversations, social observations, political events and everyday life. She relished years of friendship with the Duke of Wellington, Lord Liverpool (Fact 69), and other key figures of the period. She even got to meet the infant girl who would grow up to become Queen Victoria. Historians regard *The Journals of Mrs Arbuthnot* as one of the primary go-to sources for insights into life during the Regency and Napoleonic eras.

History written by a woman is a rarity, and Harriet gives us all a different perspective on this male-dominated world.

83. No One Wanted Louis XVIII

Louis XVI was beheaded in the French Revolution; Louis XVII was his son who died in prison, having never actually ruled; Louis XVIII was the younger brother of Louis XVI (French royalty lacked imagination when it came to names). Louis XVIII, known as the Count of Provence prior to ascension to the throne, lived in exile during the French Revolution and the Napoleonic Wars. Exile took him all over Europe, including Britain, as he tried to stay ahead of Napoleon, who eventually held sway over most of the continent.

Louis' exile was hardly frugal. He had over a hundred courtiers in attendance and nothing much to do. Years of overeating rich food resulted in gout, which forced him to use a cane and, later, a wheelchair. He never led an army; he made no contributions to science, philosophy or the arts. The only reason anyone put up with this fat, frivolous wastrel was that he was next in line to the Bourbon throne, the only legitimate alternative to Napoleon. At least Louis wasn't a warmonger, hell-bent on dominating Europe – and he could easily be distracted with a plate of roast chicken.

Following Napoleon's abdication and exile, Louis returned to Paris in May of 1814 and instantly got into an argument with the senate. It demanded democratic reforms; Louis demanded the senate disband. But Louis had been installed at the behest of a coalition of foreign states. He owed these powers everything, so he was forced to play nicely.

The compromise Charter of 1814 retained the Napoleonic Code but also enshrined the king as head of state and made him the only person who could bring draft laws to the senate. It further provided for a constitutional monarchy, but not one subject to direct legislative control. However, after the allied forces left France, some of the new legislation was imposed, while other parts were neatly 'forgotten'. Twenty-five years after the revolution and years of almost constant warfare, France had gone from a monarchy, to a republic, to an empire and back to being a kingdom again. A lot of blood was spilled for not much gain.

Louis spent months trying to get his Bourbon family members back into the seats of power they had held before Napoleon deposed them all. Most of this activity revolved around Saxony, where his mother was born, and the Kingdom of Naples, where General Murat was the reigning monarch. Murat was eventually ousted and the Bourbon line was restored.

When Napoleon briefly returned, Louis' lack of power and popularity could be seen by the speed of the defections back to Napoleon's side, and Louis fled to Ghent. He had been so ineffectual that the allies considered replacing him with his younger brother, but Napoleon was quickly defeated, which meant that, once again, Louis got to rule. He was king until his death in 1824, when his younger brother became Charles X (at least a change in name if not much change in rule).

84. NAPOLEON WAS FINISHED AND EXILED

With Napoleon defeated and dethroned, France was in need of leadership. Napoleon tried desperately to have his son made the ruler, but this was rejected. He then attempted suicide, but the poison was old, and instead, he just made himself sick. Failed generals have often lost their heads or been thrown into prison, but in Napoleon's case, the allies decided on the rather novel idea of exile to the small island of Elba off the Italian coast. That is not to say that everyone was happy with this arrangement. His carriage was stopped at Avignon where an angry mob tried to drag him out and hang him. Not all Frenchmen were fans of their ex-leader.

Napoleon arrived on Elba in May of 1814. He had been given nominal sovereignty over its 12,000 inhabitants (although the island was patrolled by the Royal Navy) and ruled it as if it was his empire in miniature. He had been allowed to retain some 600 men, which he thought of as his army, but in reality, they were more of a personal bodyguard. Now dependent on allied financing, which failed to materialise, he soon ran out of money.

Meanwhile, with Napoleon safely out of the way, the allies met in September of 1814 to convene the Congress of Vienna, chaired by the Austrian statesman Metternich. Napoleon had redrawn so many borders and destroyed so many ancient regimes that there was a genuine need for calm multinational agreement on the redrawing of the map of Europe. The congress was an early forerunner of the League of Nations and the United Nations, a place where countries could come to settle borders and international disputes without resorting to war. Everyone was sick of war, so the idea was to find a balance that would ensure a lasting peace.

Strictly speaking, the Congress of Vienna wasn't truly a congress in that there were no formal plenary sessions. Unlike previous international negotiations, there were no messengers travelling back and forth to convey proposals and replies. In Vienna, the discussions tended to be face-to-face meetings among the senior ministers of the allied nations of the Sixth Coalition, but even more, it was a cross-continent meeting of minds. Obviously there were tensions: Prussia and Austria feared a powerful Russia on their borders, and Prussia and Russia did nearly trigger a war over who got which parts of Saxony. It was the allies' original intention to exclude France as much as possible, but Tallyrand, although representing the vanquished power, did a brilliant job of gaining the confidence of all participants and ended up playing a key role. He was a master politician if ever there was one.

The Congress of Vienna lasted about nine months and showed that these ministers genuinely wanted to create a new and lasting political map of Europe. Everyone assumed that Napoleon's reign was finally over, that he was yesterday's news and that he was safely confined to Elba where he was busy playing emperor.

85. NAPOLEON PANICKED THE WHOLE OF EUROPE

The authorities in charge of Napoleon's exile on Elba were surprisingly slack about ensuring that he was supervised and that he actually remained in exile. After about 300 days on Elba, with his son and wife in Austria and no regular source of income (despite the terms of the Treaty of Fontainebleau), Napoleon slipped away and landed on mainland France near Antibes. Apart from royalist Provence, he was welcomed everywhere as he travelled toward the capital, his original 'army' of 600 growing as he went.

Napoleon's escape from Elba until the second restoration of Louis XVIII is a period known as the 'Hundred Days' (although it was, strictly speaking, 136 days). This was the last roll of the dice for Napoleon. His escape and return came as a huge shock to the allies, who were still negotiating at the Congress of Vienna. When royalist forces were sent to capture him at Lyons, Napoleon confronted them saying, 'Here I am. Kill your Emperor, if you wish.' They replied with, 'Vive L'Empereur!' and joined him on the march to Paris, where King Louis, on hearing of Napoleon's return, fled to Ghent.

The Congress of Vienna declared Napoleon an outlaw, but by then it was too late. In what everyone trusted would be the alliance that would see the end of the French Emperor, the major powers of the Sixth Coalition united to form the Seventh Coalition. Napoleon quickly reformed his old regiments and his Imperial Guard. War in Europe was coming again.

86. Michael Ney Gave Everything for His Country

Michael Ney grew up bilingual, did well in school and became an overseer for mines and forges. So far, so dull. However, a civil servant's life was not the life for him, so just before the French Revolution, he joined the Hussars. For the next twenty-five years he fought in numerous campaigns and battles, rising rapidly through the non-commissioned ranks until he received his commission five years after first joining. He was wounded multiple times and was even, briefly, a prisoner of war. It was his complete confidence in his attacks that led Napoleon to describe him as 'the bravest of the brave'.

In 1804, when Napoleon became emperor, he created a number of Marshals of France; Ney was one of them, after which he continued to fight in Germany, Austria and Spain. His list of battles is one of the longest of any general of the era. During Napoleon's invasion of Russia, he was given command of the 3rd Corps, which took him to Smolensk (where he was wounded, yet again). He led the cavalry at Borodino where there were some notoriously well-defended Russian earthworks. They were captured by the French, lost and finally recaptured by Ney.

Ney was seen as so important to the campaign of 1812 that in early 1813, Napoleon made him the Prince of Moscow, a hollow title, but it's the thought that counts. At Napoleon's end game in 1814, as the emperor was frantically going from one battle to another, Ney was doing the same, acting like a cross between a loyal hound and a cornered tiger.

However, in April 1814, the revolt against Napoleon

was, rather surprisingly, led by Ney, who knew there was no further point to fighting. It was one of the few occasions when he and Napoleon disagreed. When Ney heard of Napoleon's return from Elba, he tried to show loyalty to his new master, Louis XVIII, when he vowed that he would bring him to the king in 'an iron cage'.

But there was simply too much history between the emperor and the marshal, and when they met in mid-March of 1815, Ney forgot about the cage and became Napoleon's right-hand man once more. Ney brought all his men to Napoleon's aid at the very moment when they were most needed. He further supported Napoleon's cause by writing and distributing a proclamation urging the soldiers of France to desert the royalists and back Napoleon. It worked.

During the Waterloo Campaign, Ney was in the thick of it, taking over command when Napoleon fell ill. In August of 1815, he was arrested, found guilty of treason and sentenced to death. His execution was meant to be an example to any of Napoleon's other marshals who might think of wavering in their loyalty to Louis. Ney protested that he had fought hundreds of battles for France and never one against her. Having secured the right to give the order to the firing squad, his final word was 'Fire!'

87. The Seventh Coalition Was the Last … Honest!

While the Congress of Vienna was still in session, Napoleon escaped from Elba. The timing might seem a little odd: all his enemies were together and could, in theory, quickly come up with a response. Why not wait until the congress had disbanded?

Napoleon read the situation very differently. He devoured every scrap of news from France and Austria and was well informed about current events. A prisoner exchange had been agreed, which meant that tens of thousands of his veteran troops had returned to France, loyal warriors whose support Napoleon assumed he could count on. Then there was the news that Louis XVIII was anything but a popular new ruler, and there was also widespread resentment as some of the exiled aristocrats returned to France and tried to pretend the previous twenty-five years hadn't happened. Finally, the bickering and occasional sabre rattling among the allies in Vienna allowed Napoleon to assume that he could count on the selfishness of the individual powers to stop any effective response to his return. This assumption was one of the biggest strategic errors of his entire career.

Napoleon's return, rather than dividing the allies, proved to be the uniting catalyst that galvanised the congress into action. Differences were instantly put to one side as Austria, Russia, Prussia and Britain each agreed to put 150,000 men into the field in order to stop the emperor once and for all (a phrase we have heard several times before).

The Seventh Coalition (1815) was the strongest in resolve and intent and the first one formed from a position of strength. All but the First Coalition had been created in response to humiliating defeats at the hands of Napoleon and/or France, usually with one of the major powers hamstrung by treaties and/or defeats, which left them unable to join in the fight against the French. This time, however, all the major European powers could mobilise. They were joined by a long list of smaller European powers as virtually the whole of Europe came together in a common cause (a scenario today's EU can only dream of). From Russia to Portugal, from Sweden to Spain, everyone – even Bourbon France – was against Napoleon and his new army.

This was the end game. The Waterloo Campaign would prove to be Napoleon's last campaign. Even if he had won it, he wouldn't have lasted much longer against the rapidly mobilising Austrian, Prussian and Russian forces. He would have had to achieve everything he had done before but, this time, with fewer troops and in worsening health (although he had nothing life-threatening, he suffered from painful haemorrhoids and problems associated with the urinary tract. Twenty years of hard campaigning had taken their toll on his body). Napoleon's chief problem in 1815 was that of resources: he had limited men and supplies, while his enemies had infinitely more of everything. His return to power was ultimately doomed to failure.

88. The Battles of 16 June Were the Prelude to Waterloo

While the Seventh Coalition could count on more than half a million men, it would take time to mobilise and march them to wherever they were needed. As it happened, the first armies to find themselves in Napoleon's vicinity were the Prussians, led by Field Marshal Blücher (Fact 89), and an Anglo-Dutch and German army, led by the Duke of Wellington. They were to be the first line of defence for the rest of Europe.

The French met these armies at Ligny and Quatre Bras in Belgium on 16 June 1815. Quatre Bras was a delaying action used by Ney to prevent Wellington from uniting with the Prussian force. This was important as it meant that, if successful, Napoleon could commit all his forces to fighting the larger Prussian army, knowing he wouldn't be outflanked by Wellington.

Wellington was caught off guard by false reports, which allowed Napoleon to engage the two allied armies separately. Wellington's forces at Quatre Bras were never at full strength; it was largely the Dutch and German units that fought for most of the battle. It wasn't until around 5.00 p.m. that the British 3rd Division arrived and tipped the numbers in favour of the allies. At about the same time, Napoleon gave Ney orders to hold Quatre Bras and pursue Blücher, who had lost at Ligny. With the arrival of British forces, Ney couldn't do both, and so Napoleon's golden opportunity to shatter the Prussian forces in Belgium was lost.

The larger of the battles was at Ligny, where Napoleon personally led an army of just under 70,000 against

Blücher, who had more than 80,000. When Napoleon heard the cannon fire from Ney at Quatre Bras at around 2.30 in the afternoon, he knew Wellington would be too busy there to interfere in his battle with Blücher.

Fierce fighting, which lasted for hours, centred on the towns of Ligny and Saint-Amand-le-Hameau. At 7.00 p.m., Blücher threw everything he had into a last counterattack, but it failed to break Napoleon's forces. Then the emperor sent in his Old Guard (Fact 40), men who had fought with him in dozens of battles over the years. They were supported by cannon fire from sixty pieces of artillery and smashed through the Prussian centre. It was around this time that Blücher's horse was shot from under him, and the veteran warrior fell to the ground, where his horse collapsed on top of him. He was semi-conscious and rushed to safety. The Prussians were forced to retreat, and it was at this point that Napoleon had hoped for Ney to appear and destroy Blücher's forces. Instead, they were allowed to retreat in good order ... beaten, but still dangerous.

While Wellington managed to capture Quatre Bras, it was too late in the day, and Napoleon had managed to win another impressive victory. However, the emperor had failed to humble either the Prussians or Wellington. Another engagement was guaranteed.

89. Gebhard von Blücher Was Known as 'Marshal Forwards'

By the time of the Waterloo Campaign, Gebhard von Blücher had a military career stretching back nearly sixty years. Although born in northern Germany, aged just sixteen, he joined the Swedish Hussars and fought against Prussia in the Seven Years' War. He so impressed a Prussian cavalry officer that he was offered and accepted a role with the Prussian Hussars, fighting under Frederick the Great.

Because Blücher was a hot head and liked practical jokes, he sometimes failed to get the promotions he deserved. In 1773 he wrote an offensive letter of resignation to Frederick the Great, who was unimpressed, saying, 'Blücher can go to the devil.' So, while Napoleon always saw Frederick as a venerable hero, Blücher had actually fought for the man … and later, insulted him.

Having ruined any chances of further serving Frederick, Blücher married, became a farmer and had seven children. However, with Frederick's death in 1786 and the outbreak of war shortly after, he rejoined the Hussars and, by 1801, had become a lieutenant general. Now aged fifty-nine, he would, under normal circumstances, have been regarded as being too old for the battlefield, but Napoleon's continuing rise meant Prussia needed all the experienced generals it could get. Blücher positively welcomed the return to combat; he absolutely loved the military life.

When Napoleon attacked Prussia in 1805–06, Blücher was at the very centre of the fighting. By then he was the archetypal 'old war horse'. He could be seen leading cavalry charges, his impetuous streak still evident in his unimaginative but aggressive tactics. As his orders were inevitably to go forwards towards the enemy, he soon became known as 'General Forwards' (later, 'Marshal Forwards'). Following Prussia's crushing defeats, he was cornered, and he demanded that his capitulation papers stated explicitly that he had to surrender due to a lack of ammunition and provisions. Nothing else was acceptable. The French agreed.

Throughout the long years of war, Blücher was to meet Napoleon six times on the battlefield (more than most generals), but he only won twice: the Battle of the Nations and the Battle of Waterloo. Even then, he was only part of the alliances, not the overall commanding officer. He was never a great general, but his tenacity and enthusiasm for a fight were always much admired.

By 1815, Blücher was seventy-two and, as stated in the previous fact, sustained injuries when his horse was shot from under him at Ligny. But he was back in action two days later at Waterloo. Today, people of his age can be forgiven for taking things easy, but in the early nineteenth century, it was simply amazing to see a man of advanced years charging around with so much energy. He survived Waterloo and entered Paris with the allies in July of 1815. He remained in the capital for a few months before age and infirmity drove him into retirement at his residence in Krieblowitz (in modern-day Poland), where he died in 1819.

90. THE SHOWDOWN WAS DELAYED DUE TO RAIN

With Quatre Bras and Ligny fought on the 16th and all the main forces still in roughly the same area, it would have been safe to assume that the next clash would be on the 17th; however, there were surprises in store for everyone.

First of all, Ney returned to Quatre Bras to fight the second round of this encounter ... except that when he got there, he found that Wellington had moved on. The challenge then was to find the allied positions and engage. However, while a brief skirmish did take place between the British and French on the 17th, it quickly faded into shadowing each other as the heavens opened and torrential rain lashed all the armies for hours.

A year earlier, Wellington had been in this very region and had recognised that a ridge with a reverse slope would be the perfect defensive position for a battle, should one ever take place in this area. Now was the time, and he positioned his forces both along and behind the ridge, located near the small Belgian town of Waterloo.

Wellington spent the night at a Waterloo inn, impatiently waiting for communication from Blücher. It finally came around 3.00 a.m. After that, Wellington was wide awake and spent the rest of the night consulting with his officers and sending out orders.

Blücher's message had been delayed while he argued with his subordinate, Gneisenau, about how their forces could effectively work with Wellington's. Blücher knew that a concentration of troops was the best bet to beat Napoleon; however, Gneisenau distrusted the British and, even after agreeing with Blücher, deliberately dragged his feet in releasing his forces to advance towards Waterloo the next day.

Meanwhile, Napoleon was unusually indecisive. Grouchy had not advanced as fast as he'd hoped, and in the middle of the night, Napoleon was seen going for a walk. He sent ambiguous orders to Grouchy who, instead of coming to his aid, continued to advance towards Wavre. Napoleon bedded down in a farm house and, in the morning, had a fine breakfast with his officers. When they expressed concerns about Wellington, the only major allied general Napoleon had yet to face on the battlefield, Napoleon admonished them by saying, 'Just because you have all been beaten by Wellington, you think he's a good general. I tell you Wellington is a bad general; the English are bad troops, and this affair is nothing more than eating breakfast.'

On the morning of 18 June, Napoleon delayed the start of battle as he waited for the ground to harden after the downpour of the previous day. This would make it easier to reposition his artillery and allow better conditions for cavalry movements. He gave Ney operational command and could be seen enjoying the June sun in an armchair, miles from the front line. It seems that Napoleon had been, once again, struck down with illness, and his haemorrhoids made it impossible for him to remain in the saddle for the whole day.

91. Waterloo Was an Allied Triumph

At the start of the Battle of Waterloo, roughly 70,000 allied troops faced Napoleon's forces of around 73,000. Although the allies were commanded by the Duke of Wellington, less than half the fighting men were British; the rest were Dutch and German, and later in the day the Prussians would join them. Therefore, while the British complain about other countries writing them out of history (notably Hollywood making the Second World War an 'American' victory, rather than an Allied one), the British are just as guilty in cases such as Waterloo. However, this does not take anything away from Wellington's skill in confronting the most gifted general of the times. Many generals had faced Napoleon with an advantage in numbers and lost.

Just before midday on 18 June, Napoleon opened the battle with an artillery barrage. At this point, most of Wellington's troops were safely installed behind the ridge he had so carefully chosen, and the field of conflict itself was not devoid of features: two walled farmsteads, Hougoumont and La Haye Sainte, became focal points for both attack and defence. Bitter fighting was seen in and around the farmsteads, which changed hands several times during the ebb and flow of the day's battles.

Around 1.00 p.m. Napoleon spotted a column advancing towards the battle. Was it Grouchy, with the rest of the French army, or Blücher, with the Prussians? Either way, although they were now within sight, it would be hours before they would be able to engage.

On a road near La Haye Sainte, vicious fighting broke out between the French and British infantries. The British buckled and the French pushed through the hedgerow. One of Wellington's commanders, Lord Uxbridge, ordered the British heavy cavalry to counter this French push. It worked spectacularly, and with British infantry in support, they drove back the French attack. (Despite its success, this cavalry action suffered more casualties than the famous 'Charge of the Light Brigade' a generation later.)

It took time for the French to reform, and at this stage, Napoleon left the battlefield to rest. As it turned out, this was a catastrophic mistake because Ney mistook the removal of allied casualties from the battlefield as a general retreat and, with no infantry or artillery support, ordered his cavalry to pursue. Wellington's troops formed into anti-cavalry squares and attack after attack was repelled, with appalling losses for the French cavalry. While they managed to capture a number of allied cannon, the French made no attempt to destroy (spike) them, so when the allies recaptured them, the gunners simply returned to their cannon and continued firing.

Ney's attack enabled the French to capture La Haye Sainte. French guns were brought up, and the canister shot they fired caused savage damage to the allied infantry squares. Wellington was, by this time, bloodied but still in the battle. While it seemed the French were winning, Wellington remarked, 'Night or the Prussians must come.'

92. Waterloo Was a Close-Run Battle

The Prussians arrived at Waterloo around 4.30 in the afternoon, more than five hours into the battle. At first their strength was hardly felt, but as the hours passed and thousands more Prussians arrived, their numbers tipped the balance in favour of the allies. Also, while the fighting had been brutal at the two farmsteads, most of Wellington's infantry was still intact, having been saved from long-range artillery fire by its position behind the crest of the ridge.

Napoleon had run out of options and was forced to commit the Imperial Guard, his elite and undefeated troops. He may have battered the British heavy cavalry and won the two farmsteads, but if he didn't defeat Wellington now, the Prussian reinforcements would turn the battle against him.

As the Imperial Guard marched past La Haye Saint, they ran into 1,500 British soldiers concealed in the grass. They had been lying on the ground to avoid taking casualties from cannon fire but were now able to spring an unintended ambush on Napoleon's best troops. The British fired volley after volley at point-blank range and followed that with a bayonet charge. Napoleon's men wavered and then retreated. For the first and only time in their illustrious history, the Imperial Guard had been pushed back on the field of battle.

This was a decisive moment and Wellington knew it. He ordered a general advance to ensure that pressure was maintained on the retreating guard. The effect was stunning, and the French troops witnessing this inconceivable event were heard to say, 'The Guard is retreating. Every man for himself!'

It was around this time that Wellington's generals came under French artillery attack. Lord Uxbridge was hit in the leg and there followed this famous exchange: 'By God, sir, I've lost my leg!' Uxbridge said, in a very matter-of-fact way. Wellington replied, 'By God, sir, so you have!'

While the Middle Guard had broken and run, both the Old and the Young Guard continued to fight on. They were finally finished off with close-range cannon and musket fire, some of the units suffering 96 per cent casualty rates. The French retreat turned into a rout.

There are two interesting footnotes to the day. Firstly, the 1st Regiment of Foot Guards, who later became known as the Grenadier Guards, replaced their hats with the fur caps of the fleeing Imperial Guard. In honour of their contribution to the battle, this headgear is still worn by the regiment today. Secondly, Napoleon's cloak, left behind in his hasty retreat, can today be found on display in Windsor Castle.

Wellington described the battle as 'The nearest run thing you ever saw in your life.' More poignantly, on viewing the battlefield where a total of 60,000 are estimated to have been killed or wounded in a single day (the equivalent to the British losses on the first day of the Somme), Wellington observed, 'Nothing except a battle lost can be half so melancholy as a battle won.'

93. THE BATTLE OF WAVRE WAS FOUGHT AS WATERLOO RAGED

The Battle of Wavre is a poor cousin to the much more important Battle of Waterloo. This is unsurprising as a little over 30,000 French, led by Marshal Grouchy, faced 17,000 Prussians, led by von Thielmann and von Clausewitz (who went on to become a famous military theorist). The entire battle was smaller than either army a few miles down the road at Waterloo. However, to forget this battle is to ignore an important 'what if' in history.

The previous fact had a quote from Wellington stating how close the Battle of Waterloo had been. Had the Prussians not engaged the larger French force and had Grouchy understood the urgency of Napoleon's need for his army, then there could have been 30,000 more French troops at Waterloo. Would this have been enough to win the battle? Probably. Enough to win the war? Definitely not.

Even if Napoleon had won at Waterloo, he would have lost in the long run as Russia, Britain, Austria and Prussia would have sent more and more troops to confront him. In a war of resources, it was France versus the rest of Europe – and that could never have meant anything but annihilation for Napoleon.

The opening cannon fire that announced the start of the Battle of Waterloo could be heard at Wavre, where Grouchy had the famous discussion with his generals about 'marching to the sounds of the guns'. However, almost as soon as he heard the sounds, reports came in of a Prussian army close by. Hindsight is a dangerous way to assess past actions. It's worth remembering that Grouchy had been ordered to pursue the Prussians, and just a few days earlier, Napoleon had given Ney a dressing down for not following his orders. For Grouchy to disobey an order on the chance that Napoleon would need all the help he could get was a ridiculous notion in the mind of a French marshal in 1815. What if he turned up to help, only to discover that Napoleon had won? Would Napoleon have been pleased that his marshal had disobeyed a direct order and allowed a force of 17,000 Prussians to go unmolested?

As it was, the Battle of Wavre was very different to Waterloo. The main action centred on French attempts to take a bridge under heavy fire. The Prussians eventually had to relinquish it due to the sheer ferocity of the French attack and its weight in numbers. From the bridge, the battle moved into the town, where there was close-quarters street-to-street fighting. By the end of the battle (which lasted until the next morning), the Prussians were forced to retreat. Both sides suffered roughly similar casualties, but the French had won. The Prussians had, inadvertently, done a vital job of stopping much-needed French reinforcements from ever reaching the main battle just 10 miles (or a few hours' march) away.

Wavre was the final French victory in this long period of war.

94. Waterloo Was Not the Final Battle Against France

Wars are messy. Therefore, it shouldn't come as any surprise that there is no neat ending to this period of warfare. Waterloo was undeniably the most pivotal battle of this campaign, and it shattered Napoleon's authority. Less than a week after the battle, Napoleon abdicated. But the fighting had been in Belgium, and the race was now on to get to the French capital to ensure an allied army was present to oversee the dismantling of Napoleonic power and the return of Louis XVIII.

The French, however, didn't see things in quite the same way. They had over 100,000 troops in the area, and French General Vandamme led part of that army out to meet the approaching Prussians at a small town to the south of Paris. Wellington's forces were also on their way, so quite what Vandamme was hoping to achieve is uncertain. He might not have been able to win in the long term, but in the short term, he'd be damned if he'd allow Blücher to march to the capital without a fight.

The allies had come in a southerly direction because Paris's main defences had been constructed north of the Seine. The battle was a Prussian/French affair because Vandamme chose to attack Blücher, rather than Wellington. Battle commenced on 2 July 1815 around the town of Issy and the commanding heights of Meudon. That night a council in Paris discussed whether it was time to surrender – or not; however, it was Davout (Fact 51), one of Napoleon's most loyal and talented marshals, who dug in his heels and insisted that Vandamme should try to oust the Prussians from their position.

The next day the French attacked the Prussians (who by now had barricaded themselves in) with artillery fire. Then the French infantry advanced. After fierce fighting, the French were driven back, only to regroup and try to break the Prussians once more. This attempt also failed, and for the rest of the day, the French alternated between pounding the Prussians with cannon fire and then surging forwards with an infantry assault. But the French never threw everything they had into any assault. Vandamme, for reasons unknown, never fully committed to the battle, and because of this, while Prussian casualties were high, they were able to hold their positions. Ultimately, the French were forced to retreat back to Paris.

The Prussians pursued Vandamme's retreating men, and some forward units even clashed with the French rearguard in the Parisian suburbs. This was quickly followed by a unilateral French ceasefire, and by now Wellington had linked up with Blücher. Allied negotiators met French representatives at the Palace of St Cloud, chosen as a relatively neutral location. It was here that Paris formally surrendered in a hastily created document now rather formally known as 'The Convention of St. Cloud'. Ironically, the palace was destroyed by German troops the next time the Prussians attacked Paris in 1870.

95. After More than a Quarter of a Century, Peace at Last!

The 'Final Act' of the Congress of Vienna was signed nine days before the Battle of Waterloo; however, the aggregate effect of twenty-five years of war was such that while some powers still mistrusted each other, there would be no major European war until the Crimean conflict in the 1850s. This meant that an entire generation lived in peace.

While Vienna was an attempt to solve the long-term political issues, the Treaty of Paris formally ended the Napoleonic Wars (over the centuries there have been twenty-eight agreements dubbed 'The Treaty of Paris': the first, in 1229, ended the Albigensian Crusade; number fourteen ended the American Revolution; the last was in 1920 and set out the terms for peace at the end of the First World War).

The Treaty of Paris of 1815 was signed by France and the main coalition powers of Austria, Great Britain, Prussia and Russia. The terms were harsh and slightly counter-intuitive: Louis XVIII was reinstated, but his government was forced to pay war costs of 700 million francs over five years, despite the fact that he had never supported Napoleon's regime. To add insult to injury, the French not only lost virtually all of the territories gained since 1790 but also had to pay the costs of the 160,000 allied soldiers still stationed in France.

After decades of death and destruction, France returned to its original borders. It was still broke and was, once again, ruled by a Bourbon king.

96. NAPOLEON WAS EXILED ... AGAIN

After the Battle of Waterloo, Napoleon fled back to France, but rather than being greeted by a sympathetic senate, he was met with anger and contempt. Napoleon had risked everything with his Waterloo campaign and had lost. He had no option but to abdicate (again), which he did in favour of his four-year-old son (again), whom he hadn't seen since his exile to Elba. Again, nobody gave this directive any weight.

Napoleon went on the run; he was now the most wanted man in Europe. On 15 July 1815, he surrendered to Captain Maitland of HMS *Bellerophon* at Rochefort. From here he was taken to England and exiled to the British-held island of Saint Helena, a tiny volcanic outcrop in the middle of the South Atlantic, halfway between Brazil and the Horn of Africa. Elba had been too easy to escape. This time Napoleon had no loyal bodyguard but a garrison of British troops and the Royal Navy on regular patrols. He was going nowhere.

Inadvertently, the British had created a unique moment in history. Most great generals and leaders either die or leave it too long before they write their memoirs. Now, one of the greatest military leaders in history, fresh from the fight, had time on his hands and the opportunity to get his version of events into the pages of history. Napoleon's writings are, as might be expected, extremely biased, but he brings to life the people who surrounded him and the times he lived through (and often helped create). He genuinely yearned to see his (second) wife and, more compellingly, his only child, but Napoleon was to never see either again.

Now far removed from the halls of power, he was missed by some and still wistfully referred to by many. There were a couple of plots to try and free him, but they came to nothing. Some French veterans in America wanted him to create a new empire there, and even Thomas Cochrane (Facts 30 and 61) toyed with the idea of letting him loose in South America, where Chile and Brazil had begun their fights for independence.

Sir Hudson Lowe was appointed Governor of Saint Helena and was, therefore, the gaoler of the most famous prisoner in the world. They did not get along. Napoleon preened and demanded the respect his believed his reputation deserved (he had a point); Lowe countered that Napoleon was a prisoner and a potential threat to Britain and that he had to take the necessary precautions (he had a point).

Napoleon's writings regularly referenced Lowe, and it's clear he loathed him. As Napoleon's health deteriorated, he blamed Lowe for his enforced house arrest. Some believe that Lowe may have been poisoning Napoleon, but that is generally regarded as being highly unlikely. In February of 1821, Napoleon fell gravely ill and died on 5 May 1821, aged fifty-one. The official autopsy recorded stomach cancer (the illness that had killed his father) as the cause of death.

97. NAPOLEON'S FAMILY ROSE AND FELL WITH HIM

The fate of Napoleon's immediate family was, unsurprisingly, linked to his own. After his first exile, his second wife, Marie-Louise, was 'escorted' by an Austrian noble, Count Adam von Neipperg. He was dynamic and handsome; she was vulnerable ... and eventually lured away from her strangely earnest relationship with Napoleon. She fell in love with von Neipperg, and they were married in due course. As a result, Napoleon II was raised by Austrians and never knew his father. But there was clearly something in the DNA because the boy excelled at his military academy and later joined the Austrian army. Because everyone was nervous about cultivating a successor to the father, he was never given any opportunities to prove his ability. Regardless, any perceived threat was cut short when he died of tuberculosis at the age of twenty-one.

After Napoleon's abdication in 1815, his mother moved to Rome, where she remained until her death at the age of eighty-five. She had outlived her husband by nearly fifty years. On hearing the news of the death of her son and then of her grandson, her health deteriorated and she became blind. She had been born in Corsica and had grown up speaking Italian, but despite all her years in France, where her son was the French Emperor, she never bothered to learn French.

Jerome Bonaparte, Napoleon's youngest brother, was to go on to be the most politically active of the male siblings, thanks largely to the help of his powerful nephew (Louis' son), who would become Napoleon III. Jerome had been King of Westphalia and had supported Napoleon in his attempt to re-establish his powerbase during the 'Hundred Days'. Unsurprisingly, the Congress of Vienna didn't recognise his title, and like the other Bonaparte siblings, he was forced into a hasty exile to Italy. Jerome had a weakness for the ladies, and on top of his many affairs, he married three times.

With the creation of the Second French Republic (there have been five since the 1790s) in the late 1840s, Jerome's political luck changed. When his nephew became president, he was made Governor of Les Invalides, where Napoleon I was reburied (more on that in the next fact). When the monarchy was restored, yet again, his nephew evolved from president to Emperor Napoleon III, and Jerome became his heir presumptive until Napoleon III produced a son. Jerome was a Marshal of France and later served as President of the Senate.

As for Napoleon's sisters, it is a sad reflection on the status of women at the time that the most that can be said of them is that they all married well. Had it not been for their brother's rise and unprecedented successes, they might have expected, at best, to have married various members of Corsica's tiny aristocratic community. Like their brothers, they all, invariably, took a hit on their titles.

The Bonaparte gene pool is in rude good health in many countries in Europe today.

98. NAPOLEON WAS BURIED THREE TIMES

When Napoleon died in 1821, there was no choice but to bury him on Saint Helena. And there his body remained for nineteen years, his presumed final resting place having been chosen for the nearby spring and some weeping willows. In a way it was appropriate that a man who had been born on a relatively obscure island on the edge of one continent should later be buried on a relatively obscure island on the edge of another continent. However, King Louis-Philippe of France disagreed, and there was increasing popular demand to bring him 'home' to France (even though Napoleon was not French).

So Saint Helena was not to be Napoleon's final resting place, and he was disinterred. Both French and British onlookers opened the coffin to find a remarkably well-preserved body, dressed in his uniform, Napoleon's hat on his head. The remains were resealed and taken aboard the strangely named French naval vessel *Belle Poule* ('Beautiful Hen'), where a coffin, draped in black silk, rested in a chapel built for this specific purpose.

The small fleet returned to France with such speed that the whole of Paris was mobilised to get the city and the funeral arrangements ready in time. Huge crowds turned out to watch the procession that escorted Napoleon's coffin to Les Invalides (originally built by Louis XIV as a hospital and home for disabled soldiers). The state funeral, raw with emotion, was a fitting end to a great man's career.

Napoleon's body was given a temporary burial until his tomb was finally finished twenty years later. He was interred for a third and truly final time on 2 April 1861, under the Dôme des Invalides, now a famous

Paris landmark. While the tomb was not of his design, it reflects the image of grandeur that he cultivated in his lifetime and is elaborately decorated with hand carvings. Made from blocks of red quartzite, placed on a green granite base, his sarcophagus contains six coffins, one inside the other, each made from a different wood.

The surrounding pictures of Napoleon show him as a handsome classical god, clad in a toga and wearing a laurel wreath. Napoleon looked nothing like this, but then again, most of the contemporary paintings of the man manifest his military genius into physical perfection, rather than portraying the reality of a somewhat average-looking man. Surrounding the tomb are twelve 'Victories' (statues), symbolising Napoleon's major military campaigns and his eight famous victories, each inscribed in white and black marble. Nowhere in this structure can you find the words Waterloo or Leipzig.

The tomb is a celebration of everything that was great about Napoleon and, in a way, shows his greatest flaw as well. Napoleon lacked humility; hubris is what led to his downfall. By remembering only his successes and by assuming he would always win, he was the architect of his own defeat. His wars cost millions of lives and – ultimately – he failed to achieve his goals.

99. Napoleon's Greatest Legacy Was Napoleon III

In 1848, Louis-Napoleon Bonaparte, the nephew of Napoleon I, was elected the first president of France's Second Republic by popular vote. He had been a revolutionary for the best part of the previous twenty years and had faced exile in Britain after an earlier failed coup attempt. However, France had yet another revolution in 1848, and he sensed the time was ripe for his return. The politics of nineteenth-century France are notoriously complex, so let's say simply that although he got himself elected as president, when he was blocked from running for a second term, he led a popular rebellion and proclaimed himself Napoleon III (Second French Empire). A first name of Napoleon and a surname of Bonaparte had huge emotional and political power in the mid-nineteenth century.

Napoleon III doubled the overseas French empire and reasserted French influence in Europe, and while French armies once more marched to victory, it was usually in alliance with other great powers. Perhaps his greatest triumph occurred when France aligned with the British and the Ottomans against the Russians. This became known as the Crimean War, although there was fighting in many other areas, notably the Caucuses and the Baltic regions.

While the early days of Napoleon's reign were harsh, it eventually became known as the 'Liberal Empire' because he introduced many social reforms designed to improve the lot of the common man. He opened clinics for sick and injured workers, required employers to subsidise low-cost housing, encouraged the creation of insurance to assist disabled workers and worked to give girls better education. He encouraged innovators by rewarding them with prizes, one of which was won by the splendidly named Hippolyte Mège-Mouriès, a pharmacist who invented margarine (a butter substitute for the poor). Ironically, the new emperor overturned an old Napoleonic law that made strikes illegal, a law that had helped the powerful (including his uncle) ensure workers' compliance. Nowadays, industrial strikes are virtually a hobby in France.

Napoleon III modernised the French banking system, improved the railroads, introduced agricultural reforms and, perhaps most famously, ordered the grand reconstruction of Paris, carried out by Baron Haussmann. While no leader is perfect, Napoleon III ruled longer and more effectively than his uncle ever did.

However, both Napoleons were ultimately undone by the same threat: Prussia. In 1870, Napoleon III fell into a diplomatic trap that had been brewing for years, and war broke out between France and Prussia. Huge crowds rallied in Paris, happy for a chance to show the Prussians a thing or two, but their king was, quite rightly, far more concerned about the impending conflict. France still had the military mindset of the early nineteenth century, whereas Prussia was fighting a new kind of industrial war. As a result, France was humiliated by the rapid Prussian advance and encirclement of Paris. Napoleon III was captured and forced to abdicate. Disgraced by the Prussians, he retired from politics and died in his bed in January 1873.

100. WELLINGTON WAS A HERO, A PRIME MINISTER AND A STATESMAN

It is unfortunate that in a war of such enormous historical importance, more time is spent on the vanquished leader than on the victor. While there can be no question about the fascination with Napoleon's colourful life and times, he is not the right person to end this 100 Facts era.

Wellington conquered Napoleon in more ways than just military victory. He also had affairs with two of Napoleon's mistresses (only one was indiscreet enough to compare the 'performances' of the two men, but it appears that Arthur was the more pleasing), and he stayed in some of the ex-emperor's palaces.

Following Waterloo, the Duke of Wellington began accruing titles and roles like a hoarder. The whole of Europe was naturally grateful to the distinguished general, but he had his eyes on a career at home. In 1819, he became the Governor of Plymouth, and in 1827 he was made Commander-in-Chief of the British Army. By this time, politics was looking ever more appealing, and at the next election in 1828, he became Prime Minister of the United Kingdom.

Wellington was a political conservative who acted with the paternal instincts of a nineteenth-century gentleman. On the one hand, he was pro-Catholic emancipation, but on the other, he was against Jewish emancipation on the grounds that the country was Christian and should be kept that way. He lost the vote. Similarly, he tried to stop the Reform Act of 1832, but it was also passed.

However, it's the manner in which the two men dealt with relinquishing power that significantly separates

Wellington from Napoleon. Rather than clinging on for dear life, Wellington sensed his time had passed, and while he could have remained Prime Minister in 1834, he declined in favour of Robert Peel. Wellington remained on the fringes of politics for the next ten years or so, finally taking formal retirement in 1846, at the ripe old age of seventy-seven.

Wellington died of a stroke in 1852. Because of his many achievements over a lifetime of public service, he was accorded the honour of a state funeral. Inside St Paul's Cathedral in London, it was standing room only as there was such huge demand to say farewell to one of Britain's greatest heroes.

Both Wellington and Nelson are buried in St Paul's. If Westminster is the cathedral crammed full of monarchs, then St Paul's is the one crammed full of imperial heroes. It's in Wellington's tomb that there is more evidence of his differences with Napoleon. Wellington was never a head of state, so while having been both a Prime Minister and the victor of Waterloo, two remarkable claims to fame, his tomb is understated, particularly when compared to Napoleon's. But his final resting place seems appropriate for such a matter-of-fact, sometimes terse man. I will leave you with one of his lesser-known quotes:

We always have been, we are, and I hope that we always shall be detested in France.